A STUDY ON

WORK LIFE BALANCE AMONG MARRIED WOMEN IN CORPORATE HOSPITALS OF HYDERABAD

DR. P.G. SUNANDAMMA

ASSOCIATE PROFESSOR IN SOCIAL WORK
RODA MISTRY COLLEGE OF SOCIAL WORK
AND RESEARCH CENTRE
HYDERABAD

INDIA • SINGAPORE • MALAYSIA

ISBN 979-8-89233-434-1

Contents

1. Introduction....5
2. Review of Literature....12
3. Research Methodology....16
4. Data Analysis & Interpretition....21
5. Findings and Conclusions....97

Introduction

In present scenario women wearing multiple hats in their attempts to balance career and home responsibilities as wife, daughter, mother, etc. at her personal life, where the society expects her to be efficient for all roles. At the same time working women should be equivalent to the co working men. Family is her first concern where work is treated as her wish.

In development countries like USA, UK wives are treated as domestic engineer. They feel proud in helping their partner at household works. Educated working women are also holding the responsible posts and conscious about their duties and responsibilities at home and workplace.

Stress at home affects the personal and organizational performance or vise-versa. Due to overburdened with work at home and work place, they fail to perform their traditional roles which creates guilt in them which leads to low performance of their roles due to stress and physical strain.

The Healthcare sector is rapidly expanding with female doctors and nurses accounting for a large portion of the workforce. Their job entails a variety of issues which include night shifts, prolonged shifts, fewer breaks, and high work pressure. When there is a positive organizational culture and supportive environment at work and home, female medical professionals will be able to offer excellent medical care, be more efficient, and enhance the quality of patient care. Hence it is necessary to identify various factors affecting the personal and professional life of female medical professionals and discuss ways to improve their WLB.

The term work life balance is more related to balancing of work and life style. This term has emerged in mid-1800 itself. It is observed that anthropologist use a definition of happiness that is to have as little separation as possible "between your work and your play". The expression "work-life balance" was first used in the United Kingdom in the late 1970s to describe the balance between an individual's work and personal life. In this article we discuss about female employees work life balance in Chennai hospitals.

Due to privatization in the healthcare sector in India, hospitals are confronting great competition; they are confronted with a variety of

In order to create a balance between the provision and reception of health care, various strategies have been worked out which makes the industry effectively by health consciousness among people& welfare schemes (Griffin; 2010). Nurses play the major role in the healthcare industry and are the first ones who are thought about when we talk about health care and thus it is necessary that their needs have to be taken care and a congenial atmosphere is created for them to work with utmost job satisfaction and content, the result of which would be a high-quality nursing care. Hospitals employees are also affected by workforce changes due to technological advancement and high rate of competition in this sector. Changes in the work style, work culture, Family needs, and work demands are rapidly taking place which eventually increased the population of dual-earner couples, single parent families and elder care responsibilities. These increased changes can have the adverse impact on employees as well as organizational performance. Increased pressure at workplace negatively affects the work life balance, job satisfaction and organizational commitment(Kossek, 2005; Bragger et al, 2005; Anderson et al 2002).However, in many countries, women still tend to be concentrated in the lower-status health occupations and to be minority among more highly trained professionals. In particular, the distribution of women by occupational category tends to be skewed in favor of nursing and midwifery personnel and other „caring" cadres such as community health workers. Women are often poorly represented in other categories, e.g. physicians, dentists, pharmacists, and managers. The under-representation of women in managerial and decision making positions may lead to less attention to and the poorer understanding of both the particular features of working conditions that characterize much of women's employment and the health care needs specific to women. In many contexts, access to female

Providers are an important determinant of women's health service utilization patterns. An omission of gender considerations may also lead to inadequate health system responsiveness to the needs of men: for example, reproductive health services are often not set up so as to encourage male involvement. Gender analysis of the health workforce may reveal that health systems themselves can reflect or even exacerbate many of the social inequalities they are meant to address and be immune from. Work-life balance problem among Indian women nurses42 % of the estimated world paid working population belongs to women. It said that women section of gender is an indispensable contributor in the delivery of the healthcare services as they (women) comprised over 76 % of the total workforce at healthcare sector in many world countries all over the world. (As per statistics on health workforce, World Health Organization).As a third world developing country, the picture is given by India never provides an edge of good hope as in the case of women empowerment, on the contrary, it shoots up the number of cases registered on account of assault and discrimination against women day by day. The under-representation of women in managerial and decision making positions may lead to lea attention to and the poorer understanding of both the particular features of working conditions that characterize much of women employees and the health care needs specific to women. For instance, the presence of women is predominant among midwifery and nursing professionals whereas it visible that less number of women working in another category likes Dentists, Pharmacists, physicians, and Managers.

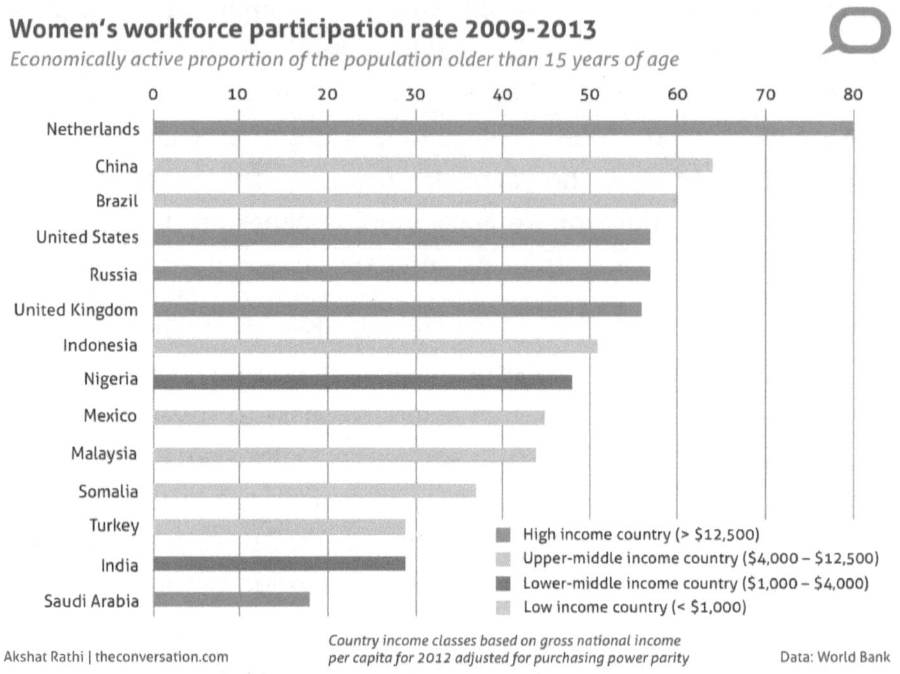

IN INDIAN SCENARIO

Indian society is at a transition stage. On one hand urge for working women at home, family think that to match their status they want an educated working wife. At the same time the bride who is highly educated is already earning and they want their wife is to look after household responsibilities without sharing their economic responsibility.

A traditional country like India, where women will not be allowed to take her own decisions related to education, work, marriage or family without the concern of father or husband. Where Globalization is an ageing workforce affects world economy, women as workers are contributing to the world's economy.

In the process of transition of society where the tradition is undergoing continuous change but the modern has not been accepted completely. There is confusion in social, moral norms and cultural standards.

There is a conflict and tension related to role play if they want to pay equal attention to their work and home responsibilities. Women who choose to combine marriage with career had to face problems in allocating time and resources between the two major responsibilities.

IN HYDERABAD

A metropolitan city like Hyderabad home for biggies like Apollo, Care, Image, Yashoda, Star, Continental, Citizen Hospitals, etc... Career and goals are become important factors in life for women. The present challenge for women is to balance the demands of family and career. Work Life Balance of Women became hot topic since the women are equally sharing economic responsibility. A married working women delivering more responsibilities like taking care of children and family.

WORK LIFE BALANCE

Work Life Balance is the adjustment of hours of individual into Professional and Personal life, which will lead to healthy and peaceful life. It gives special importance to values, attitudes and beliefs of women while balancing their work and personal life.

Work life balance, the idea of work-life does not mean that they are workaholic slave, it is a person's physical and mental well being while contributing to work being healthier and happier. Another side of work life balance is thinking that work is some sort of burden on them which leads to worst situations.

Work-Life balance is concept including proper prioritizing between "Work" and "life" .

These are some identified variables which influencing the Work-Life Balance among women :-

- Family Support
- Managerial Support
- Functional Role Stress

- Depression
- Physical Strain

FAMILY SUPPORT

Women play a vital role in their families either she is working or non-working. Working women will be taking care of the family , children and work all together for which she has to manage her timings accordingly. While playing multiple roles sometimes women will feel depressed and strained due to non cooperation of family or organization. On the other hand family expectations towards women in household works and taking care of children will be at their place and at the same time family expects financial support also. She needs more support from her family both emotionally and physically to complete her responsibilities on time with efficiency. Family should support her in work-life balance of married women.

MANAGERIAL SUPPORT

In metropolitan cities like Hyderabad , where married women also contributing equal share in economy in sectors like Institutions, Corporate, Pharmacy, Banking, etc. at different levels. In every sector at every level management support is need in various aspects.

Women into services with full time job of 8 hours working per day and 5 to 6 days in a week. Most of they carry work and home responsibilities to home but balancing between these two situations in present life requires more talent, tact, skill and caution. Women have to cope up with targets, office commitments, tight meeting schedules and the duties and responsibilities at home.

Management should support through various schemes and policies like work from home, reducing working hours and counsel them in such a way where the women should not feel depressed due to role conflict.

FUNCTIONAL ROLE STRESS

The working women are becoming more conscious and professional in their outlook. Previously they use to do jobs like nursing, teaching, and clerical but now increase in education changing the cultures, values and awareness among them. Now they are taking managerial responsibilities also which requires balancing multiple roles both at work and home.

Functional Role Stress is the stress experienced by the working women in social system. Functional Roles stress can be in many ways like Role Expectation Conflict, Personal Inadequacy and Challenges according to Pareek (1997).

In today's world, a certain amount of functional role stress is always there. Women want to complete their work effectively at the workplace and at the same time want to attend her family roles effectively which leads to stress sometimes. It is important to cope up with the situations by improving balances between home and workplace.

DEPRESSION

Women are facing lot of hardships at home and at workplace. The set of responsibility of managing home and office lie on their shoulders and they manage it so beautifully. Sometimes due to non support of family or stress at workplace while achieving the daily targets will lead women to depression. They feel that they are not up to the mark and they are unable to manage work effectively and at the same time they feel like they are not spending much time with family. Due to these feelings sometimes they go under depression.

PHYSICAL STRAIN

A woman wake up early and hurries to complete her daily work for home and for job. The city like Hyderabad where majority of the women are placed at corporate, banking , academics. They have to maintain their timings and at the same time they have to reach their tough jobs in day to day life. Due to which normally women will feel strained

Review of Literature

Work–life balance is defined as an employee's perception that multiple domains of personal time, family care, and work are maintained and integrated with a minimum of role conflict (Clark, 2000; Ungerson & Yeandle, 2005).

Work–family balance reflects an individual's orientation across different life roles, an inter-role phenomenon (Marks and MacDermid, 1996). Work-life balance is a key issue in all types of employment as dual-career families have become common and high work demands with long working hours have become the norm. The importance of helping employees achieve a balance between the demands of their work and their home lives has been emphasized. Demographic changes as seen in the increasing number of women in the workplace and dual career families have generated an increasingly diverse workforce and a greater need of employees to balance their work and non-work lives (Bharat, 2003; Komarraju, 1997; Rajadhyaksha & Bhatnagar, 2000; Ramu, 1989; Sekharan, 1992).

The knowledge economy has created greater access for women coupled with factors such as changes in marital patterns and smaller families. This has led to an increase in the number of working women and, hence, working mothers (Grossman, 1981). The gift of this knowledge era for women is occupational opportunity and mobility. But this gift has become a great challenge for the working women of today as they are not only exposed to the same working environment as men but in turn are also exposed to the pressures created by the multiple role demands and conflicting expectations. "By fulfilling their economic needs, employment has no doubt made women independent with an identifiable social status but it has also made them to juggle into two main domains of life-work and family. They have stepped into work place but the role responsibilities of women still remain the same, i.e., women may be a top executive, still the "nurturing" or "care giving" roles are considered much a part of feminine roles." (Sunita Malhotra & Sapna Sachdeva, 2005).

The study by Francene Sussner Rodgers (1992) with the sample consisting of employees of 20 Fortune 500 companies; 28 percent of the men and 53 percent of the women reported that work-family stress affected their ability to concentrate at work hence revealing that more than half the women and almost a third of the men reported that work/family stress affected their ability to concentrate on the job. Life at work seems so difficult for working women.

Pleck's (1977) research suggests that family-to-work spill-over is stronger for women and the work-to-family spill-over is stronger for men. Research suggests that female respondents in all parts of the world are pressured for time, rarely have time to relax and feel stressed and overworked most of the time, but women in emerging countries feel the strain even more so than women in developed countries. Women in India (87%) are most stressed/pressured for time (Nielsen Survey, June 2011). Several studies have explained the effect of work-life conflict on the health of working women. ASSOCHAM's study based on the survey of 103 corporate female employees from 72 various companies/organizations across 11 broad sectors of the economy focused on the issues of corporate female employees. One of their significant finding is that high psychological job demands like long working hours, working under deadlines, without clear direction leads 75 percent of the working females suffer depression or general anxiety disorder than those women with lowest level of psychological job demands (Nusrat Ahmad, March 2009).

Striking a perfect balance between personal life and professional life is becoming near to impossible. There is real balance only when the individual feels that she has done justice to all her roles and is satisfied about it. Work-life balance problems can be really serious and needs to be addressed in due time. In the renowned book, 'Work and Family: Allies or Enemies', Friedman and Greenhaus (2000) argue that conflict between work and family has real consequences. It significantly affects the quality of family life and career attainment of both men and women. The consequences for women may include serious constraints on career choices, limited opportunity for career advancement and success in their work-role, and the need to choose between two apparent opposites—an active and satisfying career, or marriage, children, and a happy family life. Work and family balance, in a way, deals with the role balance of an individual both at home and work.

Work-Life Balance Programs (WLBPs) developed by employee friendly organizations can be a good solution to solve the problems of work-life balance. WLBPs have been found to increase employee control over time and place of work (Thomas & Ganster, 1995) and reduced work-family conflict (Kossek & Ozeki, 1998) and stress (Thompson & Prottas, 2006).

Kirchmeyer (2000) views living a balanced life as "achieving satisfying experiences in all life domains, and to do so requires personal resources such as energy, time, and commitment to be well distributed across domains". The purpose of striving very hard both at home and work at the cost of her individual health and well-being for every married working woman is to have a good quality of life. But this quality of life that she craves for is often influenced by work-life balance. Any imbalance in the work and family of an individual can hamper the quality of life thoroughly for the individual.

Kofodimos (1993) suggests that imbalance—in particular work imbalance—arouses high levels of stress, detracts from quality of life, and ultimately reduces individuals' effectiveness at work.

Jeffrey H. Greenhaus, Karen M. Collins & Jason D. Shaw (2003) suggested that an equally high investment of time and involvement in work and family would reduce work–family conflict and stress thereby enhancing an individual's quality of life. And so it goes without saying that married working women of this era can have a healthy quality of life only when work-life balance is maintained making the topic of work life balance for working women, the need of the hour.

NEED OF THE STUDY

This study is basically for assessing the prevalence of work life among married working women. The purpose is also to present and discuss specifically the problems of married women face in the process of balancing their work and family life.

LIMITATIONS OF THE STUDY

The sample can be collected from married working women in Corporate Hospitals.

Research Methodology

There are two methods in research i.e. Quantitative and Qualitative. Both quantitative and Qualitative methods have their merits and choice between each method is often determined by the research strategy. Quantitative research is associated with experimental and survey research where as qualitative research is associated with a variety of strategies, including action and case study research.

Quantitative study is highly structured methodology is appropriate within the positive philosophy and such the emphasis is on quantitative data and statistical analysis (Gill and Johnson, 2010). Quantitative research collects data in a standardized manner, and seeks to examine relationships between variables.

For this study seven key variables are there, namely Family Support, Managerial Support, Functional Role Stress Scale, Depression, Physical Strain and Work-Life Balance Satisfaction.

DEFINITIONS

Family Support

Work and family are the two most important domains in a person's life and their interface has been the object of study for researchers world-wide. There is a felt need to balance and integrate family needs and career requirements Sturges & Guest, 2004 and research in the field of work–family interface has increased dramatically in the past two decades Frone, Yardley, & Markel, 1997.

Managerial Support

The role of workplace support, i.e., the support received from supervisors and co-workers and managers Voydanoff, 2002 is another critical element of work–family balance. Research shows that flexible work arrangements allow individuals to integrate work and family responsibilities in time and space and are instrumental in achieving a healthy work and family balance Bond, Galinsky,1983

Role conflict

Role conflict occurs when there are incompatible demands placed upon an employee such that compliance with both would be difficult.[1] We experience role conflict when we find ourselves pulled in various directions as we try to respond to the many statuses we hold. Role conflict can be something that can be for either a short period of time, or a long period of time, and it can also be connected to situational experiences.

Depression

Depression is a state of low mood and aversion to activity that can affect a person's thoughts, behavior, feelings and sense of well-being. For this study this definition is taken to measure the level of depression among working women due to role conflict.

Physical Strain

Physical Strain is an act of straining or the condition of being strained. The reasons could be excessive tension or stress. For this study this scale is taken to measure the level of physical strain due to role conflict and depression.

OPERATIONAL DEFINITIONS

Family Support

Family support means it could be in many ways. The women will be working around the clock and try to fulfill her household duties and at the same time working responsibilities also. Sometimes it will be like unmanageable conditions where she needs the family support in kind of helping her in kitchen, encouraging her to complete office work efficiently, helping her in household works, etc.

Managerial Support

Managerial Support plays a vital role for work-life balance among women. At workplace the women should fee comfort and should be able to adjust with the environment of the organization, for which managerial support is needed. It could be in sort of Perks, Increments, Less Working Hours, Low pressure, etc.

Role conflict

Role conflict rises where the person is not able to justify their different roles. A married working women plays several roles at home and at work place. She has to play different roles like wife, mother, daughter-in-law, manager, etc. Where the societal expectations towards women are different and work place expectations will be different. While doing these roles sometimes could not be able to justify any one role which leads to conflict. For example if her working hours are from 12 hours to 15 hours , they naturally she could not spend more time with the family which may lead to role conflict.

Depression

To balance the work and life sometimes women will go under depression. It means she feels like she could not reach the goal. And at the same time women may feel that she is not able to give her 100% to her family or towards her work.

Physical Strain

Women have to wake up early, finish the household works and should be ready to deliberate her services at workplace. Women in this fast track sometimes physically strained due to running around to fulfill the responsibilities.

OBJECTIVES

1. To study the relation between family support and work life satisfaction among married women.
2. To study how managerial functioning support women in work life satisfaction.
3. To study the functional role stress among married women and how it influences work- life satisfaction.

HYPOTHESIS

The term hypothesis can be defined as answers of research questions which are yet to be tested.

- There is strong relation between family support and work life satisfaction
- High Managerial support indicates low level of depression and physical strain.
- Low functional role stress indicates to high work-life satisfaction.
- The low working hours indicates to high work-life satisfaction.

RESEARCH DESIGN

In this study work-life satisfaction among married women as dependent variables and studied in relation to set of working hours, No. of Children and Age of the respondents. Some Characteristics identified were family support, managerial support, Depression, Physical Strain and Role conflict of Women were considered as independent variables for this study.

THE POPULATION AND THE SAMPLE

Sample size determination is difficult task in social science research. It is hard to ascertain the size of the sample. It can be determine through the representative sampling procedure based on Krejcie and Morgan (1970). For this study the researcher collected 60 samples through following the non-probability sample i.e. simple random sample.

TOOLS OF DATA COLLECTION

For this study data was collected by directly interviewing the working women at their places. The first part of the questions was related to personal profile i.e. working hours, occupation and age to understand the profile of the respondents. Questions on work-life satisfaction were Depression, Physical Strain and Role conflict. The second half of the questionnaire consisted of research instruments (standardized rating scales) to measure the dependent and independent variables.

DATA COLLECTION

The English version of the interview schedule for data collection was used. The respondents filled the questionnaire. Collecting data from working women took long time, as they were busy in their day to day roles.

DATA ANALYSIS

After collection the data the codebook was prepared . Using the Statistical Package for Social Sciences .Using the software, statistical analysis of the data was performed. Statistical methods were used for describing and analysing data and for making decisions or inferences about phenomena represented by the data. Both descriptive and inferential statistics were utilised to summarise and organise data for interpreting the data. Univeriate frequency tables were taken to check the proportions or percentages. Bivariate Analysis done by preparing through cross tabulation, by applying Chi-square test to examine the association between the variables.

PROFILE OF THE RESPONDENTS

The working women in this study belong to variety of social classes, communities and cultures. The analysis of data presents about the working women which was distributed as age, occupation and work experience.

Data Analysis & Interpretition

FREQUENCIES : INDEPENDENT VARIABLES

AGE

TABLE NO. 1

Age of the Respondent	**Frequencies**	**Percentage**
MIDDLE AGE (24 YRS TO 41 YRS.)	42	70.0
OLD AGE (MORETHAN 41 YRS.)	18	30.0
Total	**60**	**100.0**

The above table shows that among 60 respondents, 42 (70 percentage) respondents belong to middle age group and 18 (30 percentage) respondents belong to 41 yrs and above.

AGE

The idea that families have a single male breadwinner has vanished and we can see a paradigm shift in the definition of family itself. Dual earner couples, single parents, commuter marriages and break down of the joint family concept in Asian countries have caused a great shift. The employee of today has several responsibilities', towards the family, towards the organisation, towards their social interest and towards society as well. In the entire cycle sometimes, employees forget or lose the responsibility they have towards themselves. However the organizational perspective of work life balance is varied. It is difficult to establish the right balance between work and family in the healthcare sector. And the women above 40 years age have more family , work and her personal health care responsibilities.

EDUCATION QUALIFICATION

TABLE NO. 2

Education Qualification	**Frequencies**	**Percentage**
POST GRADUATE	45	75.0
GRADUATE	15	25.0
Total	**60**	**100.0**

The above table shows that among 60 respondents, 45 (75 percentage) respondents belong to Post Graduates and 15 (25 percentage) respondents are Graduates.

EDUCATION QUALIFICATION

Traditionally, the term healthcare was synonymous with hospital set-ups which meant hustling, sleepless nights, 12+ hours shift, and lack of work-life balance. Today that's not the case, we do have long shifts for nurses and doctors and the hospitals are busier than ever but the term "healthcare" is no more synonym the doctors and hospitals alone.

It is an industry in itself today, more structured, more diverse, and with more opportunities with a much better work-life balance which is possible primarily because of the technological intervention that has made it easier for people to manage and plan their work in a much more efficient manner.

healthcare is at a very exciting transitional phase where more highly educated are working, technology is helping reduce a lot of manual labor, thus, assisting people to save and manage time much more productively whether it is the introduction of more sophisticated research tools allowing researchers to complete their tedious research work in comparatively less duration or advent of telemedicine allowing doctors to have access to their patients without having to rush to the clinic every single time they plan to take some family time, she added. the future of the healthcare sector most certainly looks much more balanced.

"Healthcare is an intellectually driven industry. Availability on a need basis comes without saying. Flexibility is not just a perk; it's a necessity where work-life balance is critical to providing quality patient care. By embracing flexible schedules and remote work options, healthcare professionals can achieve a healthier balance between their personal and professional lives," she said.

NO. OF CHILDREN

TABLE NO. 3

No. of Children	Frequencies	Percentage
.00	16	26.7
1.00	25	41.7
2.00	19	31.7
Total	**60**	**100.0**

The above table shows that among 60 respondents, 16 (26 percentage) respondents are not having children, 25 (41 percentage) respondents have 1 child and 19(31 percentage) respondents are having 2 children.

NO. OF CHILDREN

Mothers are the primary influencers of children since the time they are born. Having a working mother can mould the psyche of children and make them more attuned to gender balance. Here are the facts on the different ways working mothers positively influence children. working mothers has remained quite a hot issue in the parenting arena. People usually see working moms with judging eyes. And why people, mothers themselves feel guilty of having not devoting enough time to their children. Well! This article will give you a glimpse of how children of working moms are influenced positively.

HOSPITALS

TABLE NO. 4

Type of Company	Frequencies	Percentage
APOLLO	13	21.7
CARE	2	3.3
YASHODA	13	21.7
IMAGE	6	10.0
CITIZEN	17	28.3
CONTINENTAL	9	15.0
Total	**60**	**100.0**

The above table shows that among 60 respondents, 42 (70 percentage) respondents belong to middle age group and 18 (30 percentage) respondents belongs to 41 yrs and above.

TYPE OF COMPANY

Hospitality business in India has traditionally hired women in various positions. As it's a core service sector, women are considered as the biggest asset in this people oriented industry Looking at the current status an overwhelming majority of workers in the industry are women, various subjective cases throws the light on the fact that industries are also more inclined to fill a gender gap. Hotel companies value their female manpower and provide competitive starting, salaries, regular incentives, recognition, and many other lucrative benefits

Women are taking up active roles across most of the verticals and the title itself states that hospitality comes naturally to the fairer sex. Over the past decade be it the restaurant, serene cruise liners or top-notch luxury hotels, women have been joining the various sections of the industry with increased vigor. The contribution of women in the hospitality world has achieved a remarkable increment in recent years, and in the industry their major representation in top management positions has made their status more prominent in professional domain.

The industry has now emerged as one of the most successful sectors which is supported and managed by a female- centric workforce. In the current scenario new properties are landing up where it is becoming easier for women to get into diversified roles, as the industry also has become keenly aware of women's abilities to lead and there are examples for the female population which makes up more than 50% of the workforce. The Hospitality industry working on rising the number and profile of women by lifting and strengthening their acceptance in Hospitality business. Analyzing the positive status and frame, women are still in the industry probe to challenges that prevent them from advancing within their organizations and reaching their potential at the fullest.

TYPE OF FAMILY

focus on the mother or mother figures of the family. Using a systems approach which centers on the mother child dyad, this paper suggests a model to facilitate women/ mothers' functioning as family health managers for the well-being of children. , families are socially constructed units with one of its primary functions being to provide care to dependent members, particularly children, by providing the physical, emotional and social necessities needed for survival in the environment to which they are born 1. Secondly, most family units are socially constructed in a manner in which roles are defined with regard to gender 1. Traditionally, men are responsible for providing physical resources, such as food and shelter, and women are mainly responsible for managing these physical resources and for providing emotional and social resources to the family. Given that the main function of most families is to assure the survival of its offspring, it seems appropriate that interventions aimed at promoting child health should focus on the family as its locus. More importantly, these interventions should utilize the unique roles of women within families as a means of promoting child and overall family health.

TYPE OF FAMILY

TABEL NO. 5

Type of family	Frequencies	Percentage
NUCLEAR	35	58.3
JOINT	25	41.7
Total	**60**	**100.0**

The above table shows that among 60 respondents, 35 (58 percentage) respondents belongs to Nuclear Family and 25 (41 percentage) respondents belongs to Joint family.

WORKING HOURS

The working hours of working women in hospitals can vary significantly depending on their specific roles and responsibilities within the healthcare system. Hospital staff comprises a wide range of professionals, including doctors, nurses, administrative personnel, and support staff, and their working hours can differ based on the nature of their work, shifts, and department. Here's an overview of common working hours for different positions in hospitals:

1. **Nurses:** Nurses often work in shifts to provide around-the-clock care to patients. Shifts typically include:

    - Day Shift: Typically, day shifts run from early morning to late afternoon or early evening.
    - Evening Shift: Evening shifts begin in the late afternoon and extend into the night.
    - Night Shift: Night shifts usually start in the evening and continue through the early morning.
    - Rotating Shifts: Some nurses work rotating shifts, where they switch between day, evening, and night shifts in a set pattern.

2. **Doctors:** The working hours for doctors can vary widely based on their specialty and the hospital›s policies. In general, doctors often work long and irregular hours. They may have on-call duties and may need to respond to emergencies at any time.
3. **Administrative Staff:** Administrative roles in hospitals, such as medical billing and office management, typically follow standard office hours, which can range from a standard 9-to-5 schedule, Monday through Friday, to extended hours for hospitals with 24/7 operations.
4. **Support Staff:** Support staff, like technicians, maintenance workers, and cleaning personnel, may have fixed shifts, day or night schedules, and sometimes work weekends or holidays to ensure the hospital›s operations run smoothly.
5. **Paramedical and Allied Health Professionals:** Paramedical professionals, such as radiologic technologists, pharmacists, physical therapists, and laboratory technicians, often work regular shifts. Their hours are generally determined by the hospital's requirements and the specific department in which they work.
6. **Residents and Interns:** Medical residents and interns typically have demanding schedules that include long hours, on-call duties, and frequent rotations between different departments within the hospital.

Challenges:

- **Work-Life Balance**: Longer working hours can create challenges in maintaining a work-life balance. Juggling work, family, and personal time can be overwhelming for women, leading to stress and burnout.
- **Care giving Responsibilities**: Women often shoulder the majority of caregiving responsibilities, such as childcare and elderly care. Longer working hours can strain their ability to fulfill these roles effectively.

- **Gender Pay Gap**: Women may face wage gaps due to their working hours or the perception that they are less committed to their careers when seeking flexibility.
- **Mental and Physical Health**: Excessive working hours can adversely affect the mental and physical health of women, leading to fatigue, stress-related illnesses, and reduced quality of life.

Solutions:

- **Flexible Work Arrangements**: Employers can provide flexible work arrangements, such as part-time options, telecommuting, or compressed workweeks, to help women manage their working hours more effectively.
- **Equal Pay and Opportunity**: Ensuring equal pay for equal work, regardless of working hours, can reduce gender wage gaps and provide an incentive for women to participate in the workforce.
- **Supportive Policies**: Governments and organizations can implement policies that support working mothers, such as subsidized childcare, parental leave, and protections against discrimination based on caregiving responsibilities.
- **Workplace Support**: Employers can create a supportive workplace culture that encourages work-life balance, values diversity, and provides employee assistance programs.
- **Time Management**: Women can benefit from time management strategies to prioritize tasks, set boundaries, and allocate time for both work and personal life.

Conclusion:

The issue of working hours for women workers is a complex and multifaceted challenge. While working hours can contribute to economic empowerment and career development, they also pose challenges in terms of work-life balance, caregiving responsibilities, and health. Achieving a better balance requires a collaborative effort between employers, policymakers, and women workers themselves to create a more inclusive, supportive, and flexible work environment that allows women to thrive in both their professional and personal lives.

It's important to note that working in healthcare, especially in a hospital setting, often involves being on call or working irregular hours to provide patient care 24/7. Many healthcare professionals may work weekends and holidays, as healthcare services are required year-round.

WORKING HOURS

TABLE NO. 6

Hours	**Frequencies**	**Percentage**
6.00	6	10.0
7.00	7	11.7
8.00	23	38.3
9.00	22	36.7
10.00	2	3.3
Total	**60**	**100.0**

The above table shows that among 60 respondents, 6 (10 percentage) respondents are working for 6 hours per day, 7 (11 percentage) respondents are working for 7 hours, 23 (38 percentage) respondents are working for 8 hours, 22 (36 percentage) respondents are working for 9 hours and 2 (3 percentage) respondents are working for 10 hours per day. It shows majority of respondents working for 8 hours per day.

YEARS OF EXPERIENCE

Years of experience:

Hospitals employ a wide range of healthcare professionals and support staff, each with their own educational and experience requirements. Here's a general breakdown of the experience levels for different healthcare roles in a hospital:

1. **Entry-Level Positions:** Many healthcare roles in hospitals require minimal to no prior experience. For example,

administrative assistants, clerical staff, and some entry-level support positions like dietary aides, housekeepers, and transporters may not require prior healthcare experience.

2. **Nursing:** Nursing careers typically involve various levels of experience:

    - **Nursing Assistants (CNAs):** Entry-level positions with no formal education required.
    - **Licensed Practical Nurses (LPNs) and Licensed Vocational Nurses (LVNs):** Generally require one to two years of vocational training.
    - **Registered Nurses (RNs):** Entry-level RNs often have one to two years of nursing education, while experienced RNs may accumulate many years of experience in various specialties.

3. **Physicians and Specialists:** Physicians, including doctors and surgeons, spend several years in medical school and residency programs before they begin practicing independently. This can amount to over a decade of education and training. Specialists, such as cardiologists, neurologists, and orthopedic surgeons, accumulate additional years of specialized training.
4. **Allied Health Professionals:** Careers in allied health fields like radiologic technology, physical therapy, and respiratory therapy typically require several years of education and clinical training. This can vary from two to four years for an associate degree to a more extensive commitment for a bachelor›s or master›s degree.
5. **Paramedical and Laboratory Professionals:** Professionals like radiologic technologists, laboratory technicians, and phlebotomists often complete two-year associate degree programs or shorter certificate programs. Years of experience can range from entry-level to several years depending on the specific role.
6. **Advanced Practice Providers:** Nurse practitioners (NPs), physician assistants (PAs), and nurse anesthetists (CRNAs)

often have several years of nursing experience before pursuing additional education and training for their advanced roles.

7. **Hospital Administration and Management:** Hospital administrators and managers may come from various educational backgrounds but often require several years of experience in healthcare management, which can range from five to fifteen years or more.
8. **Pharmacists:** Pharmacists complete a Doctor of Pharmacy (Pharm.D.) program, which typically takes four years, followed by a one-year residency or additional training for specialized fields.
9. **Research and Academic Roles:** Healthcare professionals involved in hospital-based research or teaching often have extensive clinical experience combined with advanced degrees, such as a Ph.D., M.D., or other terminal degrees

Challenges:

Women working in hospitals face a range of challenges at different stages of their careers, which are often influenced by their years of experience. Here's an overview of some of the challenges that women may encounter at various career stages:

1. **Early Career Challenges** (0-5 years of experience):

   - **Gender Bias**: Early in their careers, women may encounter gender bias, including stereotypes and preconceived notions about their abilities.
   - **Work-Life Balance**: Balancing the demands of a healthcare job with family responsibilities can be particularly challenging for women starting their careers.
   - **Career Advancement**: Advancing to leadership roles or specialized positions may be more difficult due to limited experience and opportunities.

2. **Mid-Career Challenges** (5-15 years of experience):
    - **Glass Ceiling**: Women may find it challenging to break through the glass ceiling, which limits their advancement to senior leadership roles.
    - **Workplace Discrimination**: Discrimination may persist, including disparities in pay, opportunities, and recognition.
    - **Mentorship and Sponsorship**: Finding mentors and sponsors who can support their career growth can be crucial but challenging for women in mid-career stages.
3. **Experienced Professionals** (15+ years of experience):
    - **Maintaining Career Momentum**: Sustaining career momentum and relevance in a rapidly evolving field can be a concern.
    - **Burnout**: The cumulative stress and workload can lead to burnout, impacting both professional and personal life.
    - **Work-Life Integration**: As women gain more experience, the challenge of integrating work and personal life continues, especially for those in leadership roles.
4. **Late Career Challenges** (Approaching Retirement):
    - **Succession Planning**: Preparing for retirement and ensuring a smooth succession plan can be a significant challenge, particularly for women in leadership positions.
    - **Age Discrimination**: Late-career women may face age-related discrimination, with employers sometimes favoring younger professionals.
    - **Maintaining Expertise**: Remaining up-to-date and relevant in their field as they approach retirement can be a concern.
5. **Throughout Their Careers**:
    - **Workplace Harassment**: Women may face workplace harassment, including sexual harassment, at various stages of their careers.

- **Lack of Support**: Women often encounter challenges related to inadequate support systems, such as affordable childcare and flexible work arrangements.
- **Workplace Culture**: Hostile or unsupportive workplace cultures can persist throughout their careers.

Addressing these challenges requires a concerted effort from healthcare organizations, policymakers, and society as a whole. Strategies to support women in hospitals include creating inclusive workplace environments, addressing gender bias, promoting mentorship and sponsorship programs, and implementing policies that support work-life balance. Additionally, empowering women to advocate for themselves, seek opportunities for skill development, and navigate career challenges is essential to their success in the healthcare industry.

Women working in hospitals, particularly in healthcare roles, face a variety of challenges related to years of experience. These challenges can impact their career advancement and overall job satisfaction. Here are some potential solutions to address these issues:

- **Professional Development Programs**: Hospitals can establish and promote professional development programs specifically tailored to women in healthcare. These programs can offer mentoring, training, and opportunities for skill enhancement, helping women gain experience and expertise more rapidly.
- **Equal Opportunity Policies**: Hospitals should implement and enforce equal opportunity policies to ensure that women have the same opportunities for advancement and leadership roles as their male counterparts. These policies can help combat gender bias and discrimination in the workplace.
- **Flexible Scheduling**: Hospitals can provide flexible scheduling options that allow women to balance their professional responsibilities with personal and family commitments. This flexibility can make it easier for women to continue working in healthcare without sacrificing their personal lives.

- **Supportive Work Environment**: Creating a supportive and inclusive work environment is crucial. Hospitals should actively promote a workplace culture that values diversity, encourages women to pursue leadership positions, and offers support to those balancing caregiving responsibilities.
- **Leadership Development Programs**: Hospitals can establish leadership development programs that identify and nurture female talent. These programs can provide the necessary training and mentorship to help women move into leadership roles.
- **Mentorship and Networking**: Hospitals should encourage mentorship and networking opportunities for women in healthcare. Having access to mentors and professional networks can provide guidance, career insights, and opportunities for advancement.
- **Family Support Services**: Hospitals can offer family support services, such as on-site childcare facilities or assistance with eldercare, to help women balance their caregiving responsibilities with their careers.
- **Fair Compensation**: Ensuring that women receive fair and equal compensation for their work is critical. Hospitals should regularly review and adjust pay scales to eliminate gender wage gaps.
- **Work-Life Balance Programs**: Hospitals can introduce work-life balance programs that help women manage their personal and professional lives more effectively. This could include wellness initiatives, stress management resources, and access to mental health support.
- **Education and Training Opportunities**: Hospitals can offer opportunities for women to continuously upgrade their skills and knowledge through education and training programs. This not only enhances their experience but also keeps them up-to-date with the latest advancements in healthcare.

- **Recognition and Awards**: Hospitals can institute recognition and award programs that acknowledge and celebrate the accomplishments and contributions of women in healthcare. This can motivate and inspire women to excel in their careers.
- **Diversity in Leadership**: Actively promote and appoint women to leadership positions within the hospital. This not only serves as an example for other women but also helps in decision-making that takes into account a diverse range of perspectives.

In conclusion, addressing the issue of years of experience for women working in hospitals requires a multi-faceted approach that involves hospitals, policymakers, and the women themselves. By implementing these potential solutions, hospitals can create a more inclusive, supportive, and equitable environment where women can advance their careers and contribute effectively to the healthcare sector.

YEARS OF EXPERIENCE

TABLE NO. 7

YEARS OF EXPERIENCE	Frequencies	Percentage
1.00	16	26.7
6.00	15	25.0
7.00	4	6.7
10.00	6	10.0
11.00	7	11.7
12.00	2	3.3
14.00	3	5.0
35.00	4	6.7
38.00	3	5.0
Total	**60**	**100.0**

The above table shows that among 60 respondents, 16 (26 percentage) respondents are working from 1 year, 15 (25 percentage) respondents are working from 6 years, 4 (6 percentage) respondents are working from 7 years, 6 (10 percentage) respondents are working from 10 years and 7 respondents are having experience of 35 to 38 years. It shows that majority of the respondents are having experience of 1 to 6 years.

FREQUENCIES: DEPENDENT VARIABLES
FAMILY SUPPORT

Family Support:

The field of healthcare is demanding and often requires long working hours, dedication, and emotional resilience. When it comes to women working in hospitals in Hyderabad, the significance of family support cannot be overstated. This essay explores the invaluable role that family support plays in the lives of women working in hospitals in Hyderabad, addressing the challenges they face and the benefits of a strong support system.

Family support plays a crucial role in the well-being and career success of working women in hospitals, especially in a demanding and often emotionally charged field like healthcare. Here are some ways in which family support can positively impact working women in hospital settings:

- **Emotional Support:** The emotional demands of working in healthcare can be significant. Family members can provide a listening ear, a shoulder to lean on, and a safe space for healthcare professionals to discuss their experiences and feelings. This emotional support can help women in healthcare manage stress, burnout, and compassion fatigue.
- **Childcare and Eldercare:** Many working women in hospitals have family responsibilities, including caring for children or aging parents. Family members, especially spouses and extended family, can share the responsibilities of childcare and eldercare, making it easier for women to balance their work commitments.
- **Flexibility:** Family support can involve flexibility in household and caregiving duties. Spouses and other family members

can take on additional responsibilities during periods when a healthcare professional›s work demands are particularly high, such as during night shifts or when on-call.

- **Encouragement and Motivation:** Family support can come in the form of encouragement and motivation. Knowing that their family is behind them, cheering for their successes and offering reassurance during challenging times, can boost the confidence and morale of working women in healthcare.
- **Shared Responsibilities:** In dual-income households, both partners can share household responsibilities, including cooking, cleaning, and grocery shopping. Shared responsibilities can lighten the load for working women, allowing them to focus on their careers without feeling overwhelmed by household chores.
- **Career Development:** Family support can extend to discussions about career goals and strategies. Family members can help working women in hospitals set career objectives and provide input on professional decisions. They may assist in identifying opportunities for further education or advancement.
- **Financial Support:** The cost of education, training, and maintaining professional licenses can be high in healthcare. Family members may provide financial support or share the burden of these expenses, making it more feasible for women to invest in their careers.
- **Stress Reduction:** Family members can actively contribute to stress reduction by creating a peaceful and supportive home environment. Reducing stress at home can have a positive impact on a healthcare professional›s overall well-being.
- **Emergency Support:** In the event of emergencies, such as late hours at the hospital or sudden shifts, family members can step in to provide assistance and ensure that everything at home is running smoothly.
- **Celebrating Achievements:** Family members can celebrate the achievements and milestones in a healthcare professional›s

career. Recognition and celebration of successes can boost confidence and motivation.

Benefits of Family Support:

- **Career Advancement**: Family support enables women in hospital work to focus on their careers and pursue opportunities for career advancement with confidence.
- **Mental and Physical Health**: Family support helps maintain the mental and physical health of women healthcare workers, reducing stress and burnout.
- **Job Satisfaction**: A supportive family environment contributes to higher job satisfaction, as women are more likely to enjoy their work when they have a strong support system at home.

Challenges:

The role of women in the healthcare industry, including hospitals, is instrumental in providing quality patient care. However, women working in hospitals in Hyderabad, like in many parts of the world, face unique challenges when it comes to receiving adequate family support. Balancing the demands of a healthcare profession with family responsibilities can be a complex juggling act. This essay explores the challenges that women working in hospitals in Hyderabad encounter in seeking family support and suggests potential solutions to address these issues.

- **Long and Unpredictable Working Hours**: Healthcare jobs often involve long and irregular shifts, including night shifts and on-call duties. This can disrupt family routines and make it difficult to be present for family commitments.
- **Childcare and Eldercare**: Many women hospital workers are responsible for both childcare and eldercare within their families. Managing these caregiving roles alongside a demanding job can be emotionally and physically exhausting.

- **Gender Role Expectations:** Societal expectations and traditional gender roles can play a significant role in the lack of family support. These expectations may limit women's opportunities for career advancement and may not fully acknowledge their professional responsibilities.
- **Work-Related Stress:** Hospital work can be highly stressful, leading to burnout and mental health challenges. Lack of family support during times of stress can exacerbate these issues.
- **Limited Maternity and Parental Leave:** While maternity leave is available, it may not be long enough to support working mothers. Additionally, the availability of parental leave or flexible schedules for fathers is limited.
- **Lack of Supportive Policies:** Hospitals and healthcare institutions in Hyderabad may not have sufficient policies in place to support working mothers, such as on-site childcare facilities or lactation rooms.

Solutions:

- **Flexible Scheduling:** Hospitals can offer flexible working hours and shift arrangements to help women workers better manage their family responsibilities.
- **On-Site Childcare Facilities:** Providing on-site childcare services can significantly ease the childcare burden on women hospital workers, allowing them to focus on their jobs.
- **Family Support Groups:** Hospitals can create family support groups or networks that provide resources, advice, and emotional support to women workers and their families.
- **Gender Sensitization Programs:** Hospitals can conduct gender sensitization programs to challenge traditional gender role expectations and promote equal sharing of responsibilities at home.

- **Parental Leave Policies:** Hospitals can implement parental leave policies that offer fathers an opportunity to take time off to support their families, thereby alleviating some of the burden on working mothers.
- **Mental Health and Well-being Support:** Hospitals can provide mental health and well-being support programs for their staff, helping women workers cope with work-related stress.

Conclusion:

In the demanding field of healthcare, women working in hospitals in Hyderabad rely heavily on the support of their families. Family support provides emotional resilience, helps balance caregiving roles, and contributes to career advancement and job satisfaction. Recognizing the pivotal role that family support plays in the lives of women healthcare workers is crucial, and society should continue to promote and facilitate these supportive family structures to empower women in healthcare to excel in their careers while maintaining a fulfilling family life. Family support is undeniably a vital pillar of success for women working in hospitals in Hyderabad and beyond.

FAMILY SUPPORT

TABLE NO. 8

Family Support	Frequencies	Percentage
LOW	17	28.3
MEDIUM	43	71.7
Total	**60**	**100.0**

The family support among working women was taken as dependent variable, the table shows that the level of family support is 17(28 percentage) respondents said it is low and 43(71 percentage) respondents said it is medium. It is observed that there is no high level of family support among married women in Hyderabad City.

MANAGERIAL SUPPORT

Management Support:

Women constitute a substantial part of the healthcare workforce, and their contributions are indispensable in providing quality patient care. However, women working in hospitals in Hyderabad, like in many parts of the world, face specific challenges and opportunities in their professional journey. This essay explores the importance of management support for women working in hospitals in Hyderabad and its impact on their careers and well-being.

Management support of working women in hospitals is crucial for ensuring a supportive and inclusive work environment that promotes gender equality, career advancement, and overall well-being. Hospital management can play a significant role in facilitating the success and professional growth of women in healthcare. Here are several ways in which management can provide support:

- **Equal Employment Opportunities:** Ensure equal access to job opportunities, promotions, and leadership positions for both women and men. Implement and enforce non-discrimination policies to prevent gender-based bias in recruitment, hiring, and advancement.
- **Flexible Work Arrangements:** Offer flexible work arrangements, such as part-time, remote work, job sharing, and adjusted schedules to accommodate the unique needs of working women, including those with family responsibilities.
- **Mentoring and Sponsorship Programs:** Establish mentorship and sponsorship programs that connect women with experienced colleagues who can provide guidance, coaching, and advocacy for career growth within the organization.
- **Leadership Development Programs:** Create leadership development programs that focus on developing the leadership skills of women in the healthcare workforce. Encourage

participation in training, workshops, and seminars to enhance leadership potential.

- **Workplace Inclusivity:** Promote an inclusive work culture that respects diversity and fosters a sense of belonging. Encourage employees to speak up about concerns, and address any instances of harassment or discrimination promptly and effectively.
- **Support for Career Advancement:** Provide opportunities for professional development, continuous learning, and career advancement. Encourage women to pursue higher education, certifications, and training that can enhance their qualifications and prospects for leadership roles.
- **Fair Compensation:** Ensure that compensation and benefits are equitable for all employees, regardless of gender. Regularly review and adjust pay scales to address gender wage gaps.
- **Family-Friendly Policies:** Implement family-friendly policies, including maternity and paternity leave, childcare support, lactation rooms, and family care leave. These policies help women balance their work and family responsibilities.
- **Mental Health and Well-Being:** Offer mental health and wellness programs that help employees cope with stress and promote work-life balance. Address the unique challenges faced by women in healthcare, including compassion fatigue and burnout.
- **Recognition and Awards:** Recognize and celebrate the achievements and contributions of women in the healthcare workforce. Implement awards and recognition programs that highlight their excellence and dedication to patient care and professional growth.
- **Clear Communication:** Maintain transparent communication channels with employees. Keep them informed about organizational policies, initiatives, and opportunities for career advancement.

- **Gender Diversity Goals:** Set clear gender diversity and inclusion goals within the organization, with measurable targets and regular progress assessments. Monitor the representation of women in leadership roles and take action to achieve diversity.
- **Support Networks:** Encourage the establishment of employee resource groups or support networks for women in healthcare. These groups can provide a platform for networking, sharing experiences, and advocating for gender equality within the organization.
- **Feedback Mechanisms:** Create mechanisms for employees, including women, to provide feedback and express concerns about the work environment, policies, and practices. Act on feedback to continually improve workplace conditions.

Impact of Management Support:

Management support for women working in hospitals in Hyderabad has several positive impacts:

- **Career Advancement**: Women are more likely to advance in their careers when they receive support from hospital management. This can result in increased representation of women in leadership roles in the healthcare sector.
- **Gender Pay Equity**: Equal pay and opportunities lead to reduced gender pay gaps, promoting financial equality among healthcare workers.
- **Work-Life Balance**: Flexible work arrangements and supportive policies improve work-life balance, reducing stress and burnout.
- **Employee Retention**: Hospitals that support their women employees are more likely to retain valuable talent and maintain a motivated and engaged workforce.
- **Enhanced Quality of Care**: A diverse healthcare workforce contributes to improved patient care, as it brings different perspectives and experiences to the table.

Solution:

- **Flexible Scheduling:**
  One of the primary solutions for management support is the implementation of flexible scheduling options. Hospitals can offer women workers the choice of flexible working hours and shift arrangements. This flexibility can help women balance their work and family responsibilities more effectively. Management should prioritize accommodating the needs of female employees, especially those with caregiving duties, to enable them to provide quality healthcare services while managing their families.
- **On-Site Childcare Facilities:**
  Hospitals can establish on-site childcare facilities or collaborate with nearby daycare centers. This would not only alleviate the childcare burden on women workers but also give them peace of mind, knowing that their children are nearby and well-cared for while they are on duty. Management support in this aspect can make a significant difference in attracting and retaining women in the healthcare workforce.
- **Gender Sensitization Programs:**
  Management can initiate gender sensitization programs to challenge traditional gender roles and stereotypes. These programs can help create a work environment that encourages equal participation and shared responsibilities at home. By promoting a culture of gender equality, hospitals can empower women to focus on their careers without the weight of societal expectations.
- **Mentoring and Career Advancement Opportunities:**
  Hospitals should establish mentoring programs and create career advancement opportunities specifically tailored for women workers. By offering guidance, mentorship, and clear pathways to leadership positions, management can ensure that women have the same prospects for career progression as

their male counterparts. Encouraging more women to pursue leadership roles can foster diversity and innovation within the healthcare sector.

- **Parental Leave Policies**:
  Hospitals can revise and enhance parental leave policies to provide extended leave options for both mothers and fathers. Supporting new parents during the critical early months of a child's life can significantly ease the transition back to work and enable women to maintain their careers without undue disruption.
- **Mental Health and Well-being Support**:
  Management can introduce mental health and well-being support programs for staff, with a particular focus on women workers. Stress-related burnout is common in the healthcare sector, and offering resources such as counseling, stress management workshops, and well-being initiatives can help women cope with the demands of their profession while preserving their mental and emotional health.

Conclusion:

Management support is vital for empowering women working in hospitals in Hyderabad. By implementing policies and initiatives that promote equal opportunities, work-life balance, and career advancement, hospitals can create an inclusive and supportive environment that allows women to thrive in their professional journeys. This not only benefits women healthcare workers but also contributes to a more diverse and effective healthcare system, ultimately enhancing patient care and overall well-being.

Women working in hospitals in Hyderabad are vital contributors to the healthcare sector. By implementing proactive management support measures, hospitals can create a more inclusive and supportive work environment that empowers women to excel in their roles. Flexible scheduling, on-site childcare, gender sensitization programs, mentoring opportunities, enhanced parental leave policies, and mental health support are essential components of this endeavor. Such initiatives will not only benefit women in healthcare but also enhance the overall quality of healthcare services provided in Hyderabad. Ultimately, the advancement and well-being of women healthcare professionals will result in a more equitable, diverse, and effective healthcare system for all.

MANAGERIAL SUPPORT

TABLE NO. 9

Managerial Support	Frequencies	Percentage
LOW	17	28.3
MEDIUM	31	51.7
HIGH	12	20.0
Total	**60**	**100.0**

Managerial Support among working women in private sectors of Hyderabad is another dependent variable for this study. The above table shows that 17 (28 percentage)respondents were having low level of managerial support, 31(51 percentage) respondents are having medium level of managerial support and 12 (20 percentage) respondents are having high level of managerial support. It shows that majority of the respondents are having medium level of managerial support.

FUNCTIONAL ROLE STRESS

The healthcare industry is a demanding and dynamic field that plays a pivotal role in society. Women working in hospitals in Hyderabad, as in many parts of the world, perform essential functions within this sector. However, these women often grapple with functional role stress, a unique form of stress arising from the multifaceted responsibilities and pressures they face while working in a healthcare environment. This essay explores the sources and consequences of functional role stress for women working in hospitals in Hyderabad and suggests strategies to manage and mitigate this stress.

Functional role stress is a common phenomenon experienced by working women in hospital settings and can result from the unique demands and challenges associated with their roles. This type of stress can affect their well-being, job performance, and overall job satisfaction. Here are some of the key factors contributing to functional role stress among working women in hospitals:

- **Patient Care Responsibilities:** Healthcare professionals, including nurses and doctors, often bear the responsibility of providing direct patient care. This involves managing the physical and emotional needs of patients, which can be emotionally draining and stressful.
- **Long and Irregular Hours:** Many healthcare positions, especially those involving direct patient care, require long and irregular working hours. Shift work, including night shifts, can disrupt sleep patterns and lead to fatigue and stress.
- **Heavy Workloads:** Hospitals are fast-paced environments with high patient caseloads. Healthcare professionals often have heavy workloads, leaving them with limited time to provide individualized care.
- **Emergency Situations:** Hospitals frequently deal with critical and emergency cases. Healthcare workers must be prepared to respond to sudden crises, which can be highly stressful.
- **Complex Medical Cases:** The medical conditions and cases encountered in hospitals can be complex and challenging. Treating patients with severe illnesses or traumatic injuries can be emotionally taxing.
- **Multitasking and Decision-Making:** Healthcare professionals must often multitask and make critical decisions quickly. The weight of these responsibilities can lead to stress and anxiety.
- **Emotional Toll:** Witnessing patient suffering and, in some cases, losing patients can take an emotional toll on healthcare professionals, leading to compassion fatigue and burnout.

- **Patient and Family Expectations:** Meeting the expectations and demands of patients and their families can be challenging, especially when they have high expectations for care and recovery.
- **Lack of Resources:** Shortages of staff, equipment, or resources can place added pressure on healthcare professionals, forcing them to do more with less.
- **Administrative and Documentation Burden:** Administrative tasks and extensive documentation are part of healthcare roles. The time spent on paperwork can detract from patient care and add to stress.
- **Team Dynamics:** Interactions and dynamics within healthcare teams can also contribute to functional role stress. Conflicts or communication challenges can affect job satisfaction.
- **Regulatory and Legal Pressure:** Healthcare professionals must adhere to numerous regulations and legal standards, which can create stress related to compliance and accountability.
- **Work-Life Balance:** Maintaining a work-life balance can be particularly challenging in healthcare due to demanding schedules. Finding time for personal life and self-care can be difficult.
- **Career Advancement Pressure:** The desire for career advancement and the pressure to continually update one›s skills and knowledge can contribute to stress.
- **Gender-Related Stress:** In some cases, working women in healthcare may experience stress related to gender bias or discrimination, affecting their confidence and well-being.

Consequences of Functional Role Stress:

- **Burnout and Mental Health Challenges**:
  Functional role stress can lead to burnout, emotional exhaustion, and mental health challenges for women working in hospitals. This can affect not only their well-being but also the quality of patient care they provide.

- **Impaired Work-Life Balance:**
  Balancing professional and personal life can become increasingly difficult, leading to strained relationships and limited time for self-care. An impaired work-life balance can exacerbate stress.
- **Career Advancement Challenges:**
  Women may find it challenging to advance in their healthcare careers due to the functional role stress they experience. Meeting the demands of their job while maintaining personal responsibilities can hinder professional growth.
- **Physical Health Implications:**
  Chronic stress can manifest in physical health issues, such as sleep disturbances, fatigue, and increased vulnerability to illnesses.

Strategies to Manage Functional Role Stress:

- **Time Management:**
  Implement effective time management strategies to allocate time for work, family, and self-care. Prioritizing tasks and setting boundaries can help alleviate stress.
- **Stress Management Techniques:**
  Learn stress management techniques such as mindfulness, relaxation exercises, and seeking social support to cope with the emotional challenges of the profession.
- **Work-Life Balance:**
  Strive to maintain a healthy work-life balance by setting realistic expectations and seeking support from family and peers. Balancing caregiving duties and professional responsibilities requires open communication and cooperation.
- **Professional Support:**
  Seek professional support, such as counseling or therapy, to address emotional stress and burnout. Many hospitals in Hyderabad offer employee assistance programs to support staff members.

Solution:

- **On-Site Childcare Services:**
  Establishing on-site childcare services within hospitals can be a game-changer for women workers. This initiative would alleviate the stress of finding suitable childcare arrangements and offer peace of mind, knowing that their children are nearby and well-cared for during their working hours. Hospital management should consider collaborations with reputable childcare providers to ensure the quality of these services.
- **Parental Leave and Supportive Policies:**
  Hospitals can revise their parental leave policies, providing extended leave options for both mothers and fathers. Additionally, supportive policies like remote work options, job-sharing, and phased return to work after maternity leave can make a significant difference. These policies should be clearly communicated to employees, encouraging women to take advantage of the support available to them.
- **Mental Health and Well-being Initiatives:**
  Hospitals should prioritize the mental health and well-being of their employees, particularly women who may experience heightened stress. Implementing mental health support programs, stress management workshops, and well-being initiatives can help women cope with the demands of their profession while preserving their emotional and mental health.
- **Career Advancement Programs:**
  Hospital management can introduce career advancement programs tailored to the needs and aspirations of women working in healthcare. These programs should include mentorship opportunities, leadership training, and networking events. By offering clear pathways for career progression, hospitals can empower women to advance within their chosen field.

- **Employee Assistance Programs (EAPs):**
  Implementing EAPs can provide women workers with access to counseling, support for family-related issues, and stress management resources. These programs can assist in navigating the challenges of dual roles and offer practical guidance for managing role stress.

Conclusion:

Functional role stress is a significant challenge for women working in hospitals in Hyderabad. Recognizing the sources and consequences of this stress is the first step in addressing and mitigating it. By implementing time management strategies, stress management techniques, striving for work-life balance, and seeking professional support, women healthcare professionals can manage the demands of their roles more effectively. Additionally, support from employers and society to reduce gender role expectations can alleviate the unique stresses faced by women in the healthcare sector. Ultimately, it is essential to create a supportive and inclusive work environment that values the well-being of women workers and empowers them to provide quality patient care.

Role stress is a common challenge faced by women working in hospitals in Hyderabad. By implementing the suggested solutions, hospitals can create a supportive and inclusive work environment that enables women to manage their professional responsibilities while fulfilling their caregiving roles. Flexible scheduling, on-site childcare, improved parental leave policies, mental health initiatives, career advancement programs, and EAPs are essential components of this endeavor. These measures will not only enhance the well-being of women in healthcare but also contribute to a more diverse, equitable, and efficient healthcare system in Hyderabad. Ultimately, the advancement and well-being of women healthcare professionals benefit both the individual and the larger healthcare community.

Print all

In new window

Types of Family:

Nuclear Family The nuclear family is a fundamental family structure characterized by a small, self-contained unit consisting of parents and their dependent children. It is often contrasted with extended families, which typically include multiple generations living together under one roof.

In a nuclear family, the focus is on the immediate family members, providing a setting that fosters close relationships and shared experiences. This structure allows for a higher degree of individual autonomy, as parents have more control over decision-making, financial matters, and child-rearing. It also provides a level of privacy and intimacy that can be challenging to maintain in extended family setups.

Financial stability is a significant advantage of nuclear families. With fewer dependents, parents can often provide better for their children's needs and plan for their future. The nuclear family is conducive to emphasizing the importance of education, as parents can provide more focused attention to their children's academic and personal development.

In urban areas like Hyderabad, where modernization and urbanization are on the rise, the nuclear family structure aligns well with the fast-paced, flexible, and career-oriented lifestyle. It allows for adaptability in the face of changing circumstances, such as relocations and job opportunities, which are common in metropolitan cities.

However, the nuclear family is not without its challenges. Balancing work and family life can be difficult, particularly when both parents are employed. Childcare, in particular, can be a complex issue, requiring external support systems and services to meet the needs of working parents.

Despite these challenges, the nuclear family remains highly relevant in contemporary society. It reflects the values of autonomy, self-sufficiency, and individualism, which are predominant in many modern cultures. While it is the prevailing family structure in many urban areas, it's important to recognize that families in Hyderabad, as in other places, may vary in terms of size, structure, and values, reflecting the diversity of contemporary family life.

The concept of a nuclear family with a working woman is a modern adaptation of the traditional nuclear family structure. In this arrangement, a nuclear family typically consists of a husband, wife, and their children, and the woman of the household actively participates in the workforce alongside her husband. This family structure has become increasingly common in many parts of the world as societies evolve and adapt to changing socio-economic dynamics.

Here are some key points to consider when discussing the nuclear family of a working woman:

- **Dual Income Household:** In a nuclear family with a working woman, both partners are typically employed and contribute to the family›s income. This dual income can provide financial stability and the ability to invest in the family›s future.
- **Gender Equality:** The presence of a working woman in the family is often a reflection of changing societal norms, emphasizing gender equality. Women are pursuing careers and contributing to the workforce, breaking traditional gender roles.
- **Work-Life Balance:** Balancing work and family life can be a challenge for working women. They often juggle the responsibilities of their job, housework, childcare, and other family obligations. Achieving a healthy work-life balance is crucial for the well-being of all family members.
- **Childcare and Support Systems:** In nuclear families with working women, childcare and support systems become essential. This might involve arrangements like daycare centers, after-school programs, or the involvement of extended family members in caring for children.

- **Economic Independence:** The financial independence of both partners in the family can be empowering. It provides a sense of security and self-sufficiency, reducing the family›s dependence on a single income source.
- **Role Flexibility:** In such families, traditional gender roles are often more flexible, with both partners sharing household responsibilities. This adaptability is essential to manage the demands of work and family life effectively.
- **Challenges and Benefits:** While a nuclear family with a working woman offers numerous advantages, including financial stability and personal growth, it can also pose challenges such as managing time, stress, and ensuring adequate support for children.
- **Supportive Workplaces:** A key factor in the success of this family structure is having supportive workplaces that offer flexible working hours, parental leave policies, and opportunities for career advancement for women.
- **Positive Role Models:** Children in such families often grow up with positive role models who demonstrate the importance of education, career aspirations, and gender equality.

However, the challenges faced by working women in nuclear families should not be underestimated. Balancing the demands of work and family life can be emotionally and physically taxing. Childcare responsibilities often require careful planning, with many working women relying on external support systems, such as daycare facilities or family assistance, to bridge the gap.

Working women in nuclear families must also navigate the complex issue of gender roles and expectations. Achieving equality within the household may require open communication, shared responsibilities, and support from their partners.

In summary, the role of working women within nuclear families has evolved to meet the demands of contemporary society. While it offers flexibility and financial stability, it also presents challenges related to work-life balance and gender roles. The nuclear family's adaptability and autonomy make it a suitable family structure for many working women in the modern world, allowing them to pursue their careers while also fulfilling their family responsibilities.

Joint Family:

A "joint family of a women medical worker" refers to a family structure in which multiple generations and family members, including a woman who is a medical worker, live together in the same household and share their lives, resources, and responsibilities. In this arrangement, the term "joint family" signifies the cohabitation of grandparents, parents, siblings, and often extended family members under one roof.

A joint family of a women medical worker may experience the advantages and challenges associated with the coexistence of multiple generations and the integration of a demanding healthcare profession into the family's everyday life. Such families often adapt and collaborate to create a supportive environment that allows the medical worker to fulfill her professional obligations while balancing the needs and expectations of the family.

A joint family with a working woman represents a family structure where multiple generations and extended family members, such as grandparents, parents, siblings, and their respective spouses and children, live together under one roof, and one or more women in the family actively participate in the workforce. This family arrangement combines traditional family values with modern economic and social dynamics. Here are some key aspects to consider when discussing a joint family with a working woman:

- **Multigenerational Living:** In a joint family, different generations live together, sharing resources and responsibilities. This can create a strong sense of family unity and support, with grandparents often playing a significant role in childcare and imparting wisdom to younger generations.

- **Working Women:** In many joint families, women actively contribute to the workforce. They may hold various positions, including full-time jobs, part-time work, or even entrepreneurial ventures. The financial contributions of these working women are often vital for the family›s overall well-being.
- **Division of Labor:** In a joint family, the division of labor becomes essential. Various family members contribute to daily household chores, caregiving, and financial management. This collaborative approach helps distribute responsibilities more evenly.
- **Childcare and Support:** With multiple family members available, childcare responsibilities are often shared among relatives. This can provide a supportive environment for working women who have young children. Grandparents and other family members can assist in childcare and reduce the need for external childcare services.
- **Economic Security:** A joint family with a working woman may provide financial security and stability for all family members. The combined income of multiple working adults can support the family›s needs, from education to healthcare and housing.
- **Cultural and Traditional Values:** Joint families often uphold cultural and traditional values. These values can shape family dynamics, decision-making processes, and the roles and expectations placed on family members, including working women.
- **Privacy and Autonomy:** While the joint family structure offers numerous advantages, it can also pose challenges related to privacy and individual autonomy. Balancing personal space and independence with the demands of a closely-knit family can be a delicate matter.

- **Communication and Conflict Resolution:** Effective communication and conflict resolution are vital in joint families. Open dialogue and respectful discussions can help address any issues that may arise due to differences in lifestyles, values, or expectations.
- **Mutual Support:** Joint families often excel in providing emotional and social support. Family members can lean on one another during times of crisis, celebrate each other›s successes, and offer a strong sense of belonging.

While the joint family structure offers numerous advantages for a medical worker, challenges may also arise:

- **Balancing Privacy**: Joint families may find it challenging to maintain individual privacy and personal space. The medical worker may desire some degree of separation or solitude, which can be challenging in a crowded household.
- **Differing Priorities**: Differences in priorities, lifestyles, and daily routines can lead to conflicts within the family. The medical worker's demanding schedule and responsibilities may not always align with the needs and expectations of other family members.
- **Career Ambitions**: The career ambitions and needs of the medical worker may not align with the family's expectations. This misalignment can sometimes lead to tensions and disagreements within the family.

In conclusion, a joint family can provide invaluable support for a medical worker, from shared responsibilities to emotional backing. While the benefits are substantial, successful navigation of the joint family dynamics often requires open communication, flexibility, and understanding among family members. Ultimately, the family's role in supporting a medical worker can be pivotal in helping them excel in their profession while maintaining a harmonious work-life balance.

Working Hours:

The working hours of working women in hospitals can vary significantly depending on their specific roles and responsibilities within the healthcare system. Hospital staff comprises a wide range of professionals, including doctors, nurses, administrative personnel, and support staff, and their working hours can differ based on the nature of their work, shifts, and department. Here's an overview of common working hours for different positions in hospitals:

1. **Nurses:** Nurses often work in shifts to provide around-the-clock care to patients. Shifts typically include:
    - Day Shift: Typically, day shifts run from early morning to late afternoon or early evening.
    - Evening Shift: Evening shifts begin in the late afternoon and extend into the night.
    - Night Shift: Night shifts usually start in the evening and continue through the early morning.
    - Rotating Shifts: Some nurses work rotating shifts, where they switch between day, evening, and night shifts in a set pattern.
2. **Doctors:** The working hours for doctors can vary widely based on their specialty and the hospital›s policies. In general, doctors often work long and irregular hours. They may have on-call duties and may need to respond to emergencies at any time.
3. **Administrative Staff:** Administrative roles in hospitals, such as medical billing and office management, typically follow standard office hours, which can range from a standard 9-to-5 schedule, Monday through Friday, to extended hours for hospitals with 24/7 operations.
4. **Support Staff:** Support staff, like technicians, maintenance workers, and cleaning personnel, may have fixed shifts, day or

night schedules, and sometimes work weekends or holidays to ensure the hospital›s operations run smoothly.

5. **Paramedical and Allied Health Professionals:** Paramedical professionals, such as radiologic technologists, pharmacists, physical therapists, and laboratory technicians, often work regular shifts. Their hours are generally determined by the hospital›s requirements and the specific department in which they work.
6. **Residents and Interns:** Medical residents and interns typically have demanding schedules that include long hours, on-call duties, and frequent rotations between different departments within the hospital.

Challenges:

- **Work-Life Balance**: Longer working hours can create challenges in maintaining a work-life balance. Juggling work, family, and personal time can be overwhelming for women, leading to stress and burnout.
- **Caregiving Responsibilities**: Women often shoulder the majority of caregiving responsibilities, such as childcare and elderly care. Longer working hours can strain their ability to fulfill these roles effectively.
- **Gender Pay Gap**: Women may face wage gaps due to their working hours or the perception that they are less committed to their careers when seeking flexibility.
- **Mental and Physical Health**: Excessive working hours can adversely affect the mental and physical health of women, leading to fatigue, stress-related illnesses, and reduced quality of life.

Solutions:

- **Flexible Work Arrangements**: Employers can provide flexible work arrangements, such as part-time options, telecommuting, or compressed workweeks, to help women manage their working hours more effectively.

- **Equal Pay and Opportunity**: Ensuring equal pay for equal work, regardless of working hours, can reduce gender wage gaps and provide an incentive for women to participate in the workforce.
- **Supportive Policies:** Governments and organizations can implement policies that support working mothers, such as subsidized childcare, parental leave, and protections against discrimination based on caregiving responsibilities.
- **Workplace Support**: Employers can create a supportive workplace culture that encourages work-life balance, values diversity, and provides employee assistance programs.
- **Time Management**: Women can benefit from time management strategies to prioritize tasks, set boundaries, and allocate time for both work and personal life.

Conclusion:

The issue of working hours for women workers is a complex and multifaceted challenge. While working hours can contribute to economic empowerment and career development, they also pose challenges in terms of work-life balance, caregiving responsibilities, and health. Achieving a better balance requires a collaborative effort between employers, policymakers, and women workers themselves to create a more inclusive, supportive, and flexible work environment that allows women to thrive in both their professional and personal lives.

It's important to note that working in healthcare, especially in a hospital setting, often involves being on call or working irregular hours to provide patient care 24/7. Many healthcare professionals may work weekends and holidays, as healthcare services are required year-round.

Years of experience:

Hospitals employ a wide range of healthcare professionals and support staff, each with their own educational and experience requirements.

Here's a general breakdown of the experience levels for different healthcare roles in a hospital:

1. **Entry-Level Positions:** Many healthcare roles in hospitals require minimal to no prior experience. For example, administrative assistants, clerical staff, and some entry-level support positions like dietary aides, housekeepers, and transporters may not require prior healthcare experience.
2. **Nursing:** Nursing careers typically involve various levels of experience:

   - **Nursing Assistants (CNAs):** Entry-level positions with no formal education required.
   - **Licensed Practical Nurses (LPNs) and Licensed Vocational Nurses (LVNs):** Generally require one to two years of vocational training.
   - **Registered Nurses (RNs):** Entry-level RNs often have one to two years of nursing education, while experienced RNs may accumulate many years of experience in various specialties.

3. **Physicians and Specialists:** Physicians, including doctors and surgeons, spend several years in medical school and residency programs before they begin practicing independently. This can amount to over a decade of education and training. Specialists, such as cardiologists, neurologists, and orthopedic surgeons, accumulate additional years of specialized training.
4. **Allied Health Professionals:** Careers in allied health fields like radiologic technology, physical therapy, and respiratory therapy typically require several years of education and clinical training. This can vary from two to four years for an associate degree to a more extensive commitment for a bachelor›s or master›s degree.
5. **Paramedical and Laboratory Professionals:** Professionals like radiologic technologists, laboratory technicians, and

phlebotomists often complete two-year associate degree programs or shorter certificate programs. Years of experience can range from entry-level to several years depending on the specific role.

6. **Advanced Practice Providers:** Nurse practitioners (NPs), physician assistants (PAs), and nurse anesthetists (CRNAs) often have several years of nursing experience before pursuing additional education and training for their advanced roles.
7. **Hospital Administration and Management:** Hospital administrators and managers may come from various educational backgrounds but often require several years of experience in healthcare management, which can range from five to fifteen years or more.
8. **Pharmacists:** Pharmacists complete a Doctor of Pharmacy (Pharm.D.) program, which typically takes four years, followed by a one-year residency or additional training for specialized fields.
9. **Research and Academic Roles:** Healthcare professionals involved in hospital-based research or teaching often have extensive clinical experience combined with advanced degrees, such as a Ph.D., M.D., or other terminal degrees.

Challenges:

Women working in hospitals face a range of challenges at different stages of their careers, which are often influenced by their years of experience. Here's an overview of some of the challenges that women may encounter at various career stages:

1. **Early Career Challenges** (0-5 years of experience):

    - **Gender Bias**: Early in their careers, women may encounter gender bias, including stereotypes and preconceived notions about their abilities.

- **Work-Life Balance**: Balancing the demands of a healthcare job with family responsibilities can be particularly challenging for women starting their careers.
- **Career Advancement**: Advancing to leadership roles or specialized positions may be more difficult due to limited experience and opportunities.

2. **Mid-Career Challenges** (5-15 years of experience):

   - **Glass Ceiling**: Women may find it challenging to break through the glass ceiling, which limits their advancement to senior leadership roles.
   - **Workplace Discrimination**: Discrimination may persist, including disparities in pay, opportunities, and recognition.
   - **Mentorship and Sponsorship**: Finding mentors and sponsors who can support their career growth can be crucial but challenging for women in mid-career stages.

3. **Experienced Professionals** (15+ years of experience):

   - **Maintaining Career Momentum**: Sustaining career momentum and relevance in a rapidly evolving field can be a concern.
   - **Burnout**: The cumulative stress and workload can lead to burnout, impacting both professional and personal life.
   - **Work-Life Integration**: As women gain more experience, the challenge of integrating work and personal life continues, especially for those in leadership roles.

4. **Late Career Challenges** (Approaching Retirement):

   - **Succession Planning**: Preparing for retirement and ensuring a smooth succession plan can be a significant challenge, particularly for women in leadership positions.
   - **Age Discrimination**: Late-career women may face age-related discrimination, with employers sometimes favoring younger professionals.

- **Maintaining Expertise**: Remaining up-to-date and relevant in their field as they approach retirement can be a concern.

5. **Throughout Their Careers**:

   - **Workplace Harassment**: Women may face workplace harassment, including sexual harassment, at various stages of their careers.
   - **Lack of Support**: Women often encounter challenges related to inadequate support systems, such as affordable childcare and flexible work arrangements.
   - **Workplace Culture**: Hostile or unsupportive workplace cultures can persist throughout their careers.

Addressing these challenges requires a concerted effort from healthcare organizations, policymakers, and society as a whole. Strategies to support women in hospitals include creating inclusive workplace environments, addressing gender bias, promoting mentorship and sponsorship programs, and implementing policies that support work-life balance. Additionally, empowering women to advocate for themselves, seek opportunities for skill development, and navigate career challenges is essential to their success in the healthcare industry.

Women working in hospitals, particularly in healthcare roles, face a variety of challenges related to years of experience. These challenges can impact their career advancement and overall job satisfaction. Here are some potential solutions to address these issues:

- **Professional Development Programs**: Hospitals can establish and promote professional development programs specifically tailored to women in healthcare. These programs can offer mentoring, training, and opportunities for skill enhancement, helping women gain experience and expertise more rapidly.
- **Equal Opportunity Policies**: Hospitals should implement and enforce equal opportunity policies to ensure that women have the same opportunities for advancement and leadership roles as

their male counterparts. These policies can help combat gender bias and discrimination in the workplace.

- **Flexible Scheduling:** Hospitals can provide flexible scheduling options that allow women to balance their professional responsibilities with personal and family commitments. This flexibility can make it easier for women to continue working in healthcare without sacrificing their personal lives.
- **Supportive Work Environment:** Creating a supportive and inclusive work environment is crucial. Hospitals should actively promote a workplace culture that values diversity, encourages women to pursue leadership positions, and offers support to those balancing caregiving responsibilities.
- **Leadership Development Programs:** Hospitals can establish leadership development programs that identify and nurture female talent. These programs can provide the necessary training and mentorship to help women move into leadership roles.
- **Mentorship and Networking:** Hospitals should encourage mentorship and networking opportunities for women in healthcare. Having access to mentors and professional networks can provide guidance, career insights, and opportunities for advancement.
- **Family Support Services:** Hospitals can offer family support services, such as on-site childcare facilities or assistance with eldercare, to help women balance their caregiving responsibilities with their careers.
- **Fair Compensation:** Ensuring that women receive fair and equal compensation for their work is critical. Hospitals should regularly review and adjust pay scales to eliminate gender wage gaps.
- **Work-Life Balance Programs:** Hospitals can introduce work-life balance programs that help women manage their personal and professional lives more effectively. This could include

wellness initiatives, stress management resources, and access to mental health support.

- **Education and Training Opportunities**: Hospitals can offer opportunities for women to continuously upgrade their skills and knowledge through education and training programs. This not only enhances their experience but also keeps them up-to-date with the latest advancements in healthcare.
- **Recognition and Awards**: Hospitals can institute recognition and award programs that acknowledge and celebrate the accomplishments and contributions of women in healthcare. This can motivate and inspire women to excel in their careers.
- **Diversity in Leadership**: Actively promote and appoint women to leadership positions within the hospital. This not only serves as an example for other women but also helps in decision-making that takes into account a diverse range of perspectives.

In conclusion, addressing the issue of years of experience for women working in hospitals requires a multi-faceted approach that involves hospitals, policymakers, and the women themselves. By implementing these potential solutions, hospitals can create a more inclusive, supportive, and equitable environment where women can advance their careers and contribute effectively to the healthcare sector.

Family Support:

The field of healthcare is demanding and often requires long working hours, dedication, and emotional resilience. When it comes to women working in hospitals in Hyderabad, the significance of family support cannot be overstated. This essay explores the invaluable role that family support plays in the lives of women working in hospitals in Hyderabad, addressing the challenges they face and the benefits of a strong support system.

Family support plays a crucial role in the well-being and career success of working women in hospitals, especially in a demanding and often emotionally charged field like healthcare. Here are some ways in which family support can positively impact working women in hospital settings:

- **Emotional Support:** The emotional demands of working in healthcare can be significant. Family members can provide a listening ear, a shoulder to lean on, and a safe space for healthcare professionals to discuss their experiences and feelings. This emotional support can help women in healthcare manage stress, burnout, and compassion fatigue.
- **Childcare and Eldercare:** Many working women in hospitals have family responsibilities, including caring for children or aging parents. Family members, especially spouses and extended family, can share the responsibilities of childcare and eldercare, making it easier for women to balance their work commitments.
- **Flexibility:** Family support can involve flexibility in household and caregiving duties. Spouses and other family members can take on additional responsibilities during periods when a healthcare professional›s work demands are particularly high, such as during night shifts or when on-call.
- **Encouragement and Motivation:** Family support can come in the form of encouragement and motivation. Knowing that their family is behind them, cheering for their successes and offering reassurance during challenging times, can boost the confidence and morale of working women in healthcare.
- **Shared Responsibilities:** In dual-income households, both partners can share household responsibilities, including cooking, cleaning, and grocery shopping. Shared responsibilities can lighten the load for working women, allowing them to focus on their careers without feeling overwhelmed by household chores.
- **Career Development:** Family support can extend to discussions about career goals and strategies. Family members can help working women in hospitals set career objectives and provide

input on professional decisions. They may assist in identifying opportunities for further education or advancement.

- **Financial Support:** The cost of education, training, and maintaining professional licenses can be high in healthcare. Family members may provide financial support or share the burden of these expenses, making it more feasible for women to invest in their careers.
- **Stress Reduction:** Family members can actively contribute to stress reduction by creating a peaceful and supportive home environment. Reducing stress at home can have a positive impact on a healthcare professional›s overall well-being.
- **Emergency Support:** In the event of emergencies, such as late hours at the hospital or sudden shifts, family members can step in to provide assistance and ensure that everything at home is running smoothly.
- **Celebrating Achievements:** Family members can celebrate the achievements and milestones in a healthcare professional›s career. Recognition and celebration of successes can boost confidence and motivation.

Benefits of Family Support:

- **Career Advancement**: Family support enables women in hospital work to focus on their careers and pursue opportunities for career advancement with confidence.
- **Mental and Physical Health**: Family support helps maintain the mental and physical health of women healthcare workers, reducing stress and burnout.
- **Job Satisfaction**: A supportive family environment contributes to higher job satisfaction, as women are more likely to enjoy their work when they have a strong support system at home.

Challenges:

The role of women in the healthcare industry, including hospitals, is instrumental in providing quality patient care. However, women working in hospitals in Hyderabad, like in many parts of the world, face unique challenges when it comes to receiving adequate family support. Balancing the demands of a healthcare profession with family responsibilities can be a complex juggling act. This essay explores the challenges that women working in hospitals in Hyderabad encounter in seeking family support and suggests potential solutions to address these issues.

- **Long and Unpredictable Working Hours:** Healthcare jobs often involve long and irregular shifts, including night shifts and on-call duties. This can disrupt family routines and make it difficult to be present for family commitments.
- **Childcare and Eldercare:** Many women hospital workers are responsible for both childcare and eldercare within their families. Managing these caregiving roles alongside a demanding job can be emotionally and physically exhausting.
- **Gender Role Expectations:** Societal expectations and traditional gender roles can play a significant role in the lack of family support. These expectations may limit women's opportunities for career advancement and may not fully acknowledge their professional responsibilities.
- **Work-Related Stress:** Hospital work can be highly stressful, leading to burnout and mental health challenges. Lack of family support during times of stress can exacerbate these issues.
- **Limited Maternity and Parental Leave:** While maternity leave is available, it may not be long enough to support working mothers. Additionally, the availability of parental leave or flexible schedules for fathers is limited.
- **Lack of Supportive Policies:** Hospitals and healthcare institutions in Hyderabad may not have sufficient policies in place to support working mothers, such as on-site childcare facilities or lactation rooms.

Solutions:

- **Flexible Scheduling**: Hospitals can offer flexible working hours and shift arrangements to help women workers better manage their family responsibilities.
- **On-Site Childcare Facilities**: Providing on-site childcare services can significantly ease the childcare burden on women hospital workers, allowing them to focus on their jobs.
- **Family Support Groups**: Hospitals can create family support groups or networks that provide resources, advice, and emotional support to women workers and their families.
- **Gender Sensitization Programs**: Hospitals can conduct gender sensitization programs to challenge traditional gender role expectations and promote equal sharing of responsibilities at home.
- **Parental Leave Policies**: Hospitals can implement parental leave policies that offer fathers an opportunity to take time off to support their families, thereby alleviating some of the burden on working mothers.
- **Mental Health and Well-being Support**: Hospitals can provide mental health and well-being support programs for their staff, helping women workers cope with work-related stress.

Conclusion:

In the demanding field of healthcare, women working in hospitals in Hyderabad rely heavily on the support of their families. Family support provides emotional resilience, helps balance caregiving roles, and contributes to career advancement and job satisfaction. Recognizing the pivotal role that family support plays in the lives of women healthcare workers is crucial, and society should continue to promote and facilitate these supportive family structures to empower women in healthcare to excel in their careers while maintaining a fulfilling family life. Family support is undeniably a vital pillar of success for women working in hospitals in Hyderabad and beyond.

Management Support:

Women constitute a substantial part of the healthcare workforce, and their contributions are indispensable in providing quality patient care. However, women working in hospitals in Hyderabad, like in many parts of the world, face specific challenges and opportunities in their professional journey. This essay explores the importance of management support for women working in hospitals in Hyderabad and its impact on their careers and well-being.

Management support of working women in hospitals is crucial for ensuring a supportive and inclusive work environment that promotes gender equality, career advancement, and overall well-being. Hospital management can play a significant role in facilitating the success and professional growth of women in healthcare. Here are several ways in which management can provide support:

- **Equal Employment Opportunities:** Ensure equal access to job opportunities, promotions, and leadership positions for both women and men. Implement and enforce non-discrimination policies to prevent gender-based bias in recruitment, hiring, and advancement.
- **Flexible Work Arrangements:** Offer flexible work arrangements, such as part-time, remote work, job sharing, and adjusted schedules to accommodate the unique needs of working women, including those with family responsibilities.
- **Mentoring and Sponsorship Programs:** Establish mentorship and sponsorship programs that connect women with experienced colleagues who can provide guidance, coaching, and advocacy for career growth within the organization.
- **Leadership Development Programs:** Create leadership development programs that focus on developing the leadership skills of women in the healthcare workforce. Encourage participation in training, workshops, and seminars to enhance leadership potential.

- **Workplace Inclusivity:** Promote an inclusive work culture that respects diversity and fosters a sense of belonging. Encourage employees to speak up about concerns, and address any instances of harassment or discrimination promptly and effectively.
- **Support for Career Advancement:** Provide opportunities for professional development, continuous learning, and career advancement. Encourage women to pursue higher education, certifications, and training that can enhance their qualifications and prospects for leadership roles.
- **Fair Compensation:** Ensure that compensation and benefits are equitable for all employees, regardless of gender. Regularly review and adjust pay scales to address gender wage gaps.
- **Family-Friendly Policies:** Implement family-friendly policies, including maternity and paternity leave, childcare support, lactation rooms, and family care leave. These policies help women balance their work and family responsibilities.
- **Mental Health and Well-Being:** Offer mental health and wellness programs that help employees cope with stress and promote work-life balance. Address the unique challenges faced by women in healthcare, including compassion fatigue and burnout.
- **Recognition and Awards:** Recognize and celebrate the achievements and contributions of women in the healthcare workforce. Implement awards and recognition programs that highlight their excellence and dedication to patient care and professional growth.
- **Clear Communication:** Maintain transparent communication channels with employees. Keep them informed about organizational policies, initiatives, and opportunities for career advancement.
- **Gender Diversity Goals:** Set clear gender diversity and inclusion goals within the organization, with measurable targets and regular progress assessments. Monitor the representation of women in leadership roles and take action to achieve diversity.

- **Support Networks:** Encourage the establishment of employee resource groups or support networks for women in healthcare. These groups can provide a platform for networking, sharing experiences, and advocating for gender equality within the organization.
- **Feedback Mechanisms:** Create mechanisms for employees, including women, to provide feedback and express concerns about the work environment, policies, and practices. Act on feedback to continually improve workplace conditions.

Impact of Management Support:

Management support for women working in hospitals in Hyderabad has several positive impacts:

- **Career Advancement**: Women are more likely to advance in their careers when they receive support from hospital management. This can result in increased representation of women in leadership roles in the healthcare sector.
- **Gender Pay Equity**: Equal pay and opportunities lead to reduced gender pay gaps, promoting financial equality among healthcare workers.
- **Work-Life Balance**: Flexible work arrangements and supportive policies improve work-life balance, reducing stress and burnout.
- **Employee Retention**: Hospitals that support their women employees are more likely to retain valuable talent and maintain a motivated and engaged workforce.
- **Enhanced Quality of Care**: A diverse healthcare workforce contributes to improved patient care, as it brings different perspectives and experiences to the table.

Solution:

- **Flexible Scheduling**:

  One of the primary solutions for management support is the implementation of flexible scheduling options. Hospitals can offer women workers the choice of flexible working hours and shift arrangements. This flexibility can help women balance their work and family responsibilities more effectively. Management should prioritize accommodating the needs of female employees, especially those with caregiving duties, to enable them to provide quality healthcare services while managing their families.

- **On-Site Childcare Facilities**:
  Hospitals can establish on-site childcare facilities or collaborate with nearby daycare centers. This would not only alleviate the childcare burden on women workers but also give them peace of mind, knowing that their children are nearby and well-cared for while they are on duty. Management support in this aspect can make a significant difference in attracting and retaining women in the healthcare workforce.
- **Gender Sensitization Programs**:
  Management can initiate gender sensitization programs to challenge traditional gender roles and stereotypes. These programs can help create a work environment that encourages equal participation and shared responsibilities at home. By promoting a culture of gender equality, hospitals can empower women to focus on their careers without the weight of societal expectations.
- **Mentoring and Career Advancement Opportunities**:
  Hospitals should establish mentoring programs and create career advancement opportunities specifically tailored for women workers. By offering guidance, mentorship, and clear pathways to leadership positions, management can ensure that women have the same prospects for career progression as their male counterparts. Encouraging more women to pursue leadership roles can foster diversity and innovation within the healthcare sector.

- **Parental Leave Policies**:
  Hospitals can revise and enhance parental leave policies to provide extended leave options for both mothers and fathers. Supporting new parents during the critical early months of a child's life can significantly ease the transition back to work and enable women to maintain their careers without undue disruption.
- **Mental Health and Well-being Support**:
  Management can introduce mental health and well-being support programs for staff, with a particular focus on women workers. Stress-related burnout is common in the healthcare sector, and offering resources such as counseling, stress management workshops, and well-being initiatives can help women cope with the demands of their profession while preserving their mental and emotional health.

Conclusion:

Management support is vital for empowering women working in hospitals in Hyderabad. By implementing policies and initiatives that promote equal opportunities, work-life balance, and career advancement, hospitals can create an inclusive and supportive environment that allows women to thrive in their professional journeys. This not only benefits women healthcare workers but also contributes to a more diverse and effective healthcare system, ultimately enhancing patient care and overall well-being.

Women working in hospitals in Hyderabad are vital contributors to the healthcare sector. By implementing proactive management support measures, hospitals can create a more inclusive and supportive work environment that empowers women to excel in their roles. Flexible scheduling, on-site childcare, gender sensitization programs, mentoring opportunities, enhanced parental leave policies, and mental health support are essential components of this endeavor.

Such initiatives will not only benefit women in healthcare but also enhance the overall quality of healthcare services provided in Hyderabad. Ultimately, the advancement and well-being of women healthcare professionals will result in a more equitable, diverse, and effective healthcare system for all.

Functional Role Stress:

The healthcare industry is a demanding and dynamic field that plays a pivotal role in society. Women working in hospitals in Hyderabad, as in many parts of the world, perform essential functions within this sector. However, these women often grapple with functional role stress, a unique form of stress arising from the multifaceted responsibilities and pressures they face while working in a healthcare environment. This essay explores the sources and consequences of functional role stress for women working in hospitals in Hyderabad and suggests strategies to manage and mitigate this stress.

Functional role stress is a common phenomenon experienced by working women in hospital settings and can result from the unique demands and challenges associated with their roles. This type of stress can affect their well-being, job performance, and overall job satisfaction. Here are some of the key factors contributing to functional role stress among working women in hospitals:

- **Patient Care Responsibilities:** Healthcare professionals, including nurses and doctors, often bear the responsibility of providing direct patient care. This involves managing the physical and emotional needs of patients, which can be emotionally draining and stressful.
- **Long and Irregular Hours:** Many healthcare positions, especially those involving direct patient care, require long and irregular working hours. Shift work, including night shifts, can disrupt sleep patterns and lead to fatigue and stress.
- **Heavy Workloads:** Hospitals are fast-paced environments with high patient caseloads. Healthcare professionals often have

heavy workloads, leaving them with limited time to provide individualized care.

- **Emergency Situations:** Hospitals frequently deal with critical and emergency cases. Healthcare workers must be prepared to respond to sudden crises, which can be highly stressful.
- **Complex Medical Cases:** The medical conditions and cases encountered in hospitals can be complex and challenging. Treating patients with severe illnesses or traumatic injuries can be emotionally taxing.
- **Multitasking and Decision-Making:** Healthcare professionals must often multitask and make critical decisions quickly. The weight of these responsibilities can lead to stress and anxiety.
- **Emotional Toll:** Witnessing patient suffering and, in some cases, losing patients can take an emotional toll on healthcare professionals, leading to compassion fatigue and burnout.
- **Patient and Family Expectations:** Meeting the expectations and demands of patients and their families can be challenging, especially when they have high expectations for care and recovery.
- **Lack of Resources:** Shortages of staff, equipment, or resources can place added pressure on healthcare professionals, forcing them to do more with less.
- **Administrative and Documentation Burden:** Administrative tasks and extensive documentation are part of healthcare roles. The time spent on paperwork can detract from patient care and add to stress.
- **Team Dynamics:** Interactions and dynamics within healthcare teams can also contribute to functional role stress. Conflicts or communication challenges can affect job satisfaction.
- **Regulatory and Legal Pressure:** Healthcare professionals must adhere to numerous regulations and legal standards, which can create stress related to compliance and accountability.

FUNCTIONAL ROLE STRESS

TABLE NO. 10

Functional Role Stress	Frequencies	Percentage
LOW	16	26.7
MEDIUM	35	58.3
HIGH	9	15.0
Total	**60**	**100.0**

Role stress among working women in Private Sectors of Hyderabad is another Dependent Variable for this study. The above table shows that Functional Role Stress among working women in Private Sectors of Hyderabad. It shows that 16(26 percetnage) respondents are having low functional role stress, 35 (58 percentage) respondents are having medium functional role stress and 9 (15 percentage) respondents are having high functional role stress. It shows that Among working women there is medium level of functional role stress in this study.

DEPRESSION

TABLE NO.11

Depression	Frequencies	Percentage
LOW	16	26.7
MEDIUM	29	48.3
HIGH	15	25.0
Total	**60**	**100.0**

Depression level is one of the important variable in this study. The above table shows that Depression among working women in Private Sectors of Hyderabad. It shows that 16(26 percetnage) respondents are having low level of depression, 29(48 percentage) respondents are having medium level of depression and 15 (25 percentage) respondents are having high level of depression. It shows that among working women there is the level of depression is medium in this study.

The healthcare industry is a demanding and dynamic field that plays a pivotal role in society. Women working in hospitals in Hyderabad, as in many parts of the world, perform essential functions within this sector. However, these women often grapple with functional role stress, a unique form of stress arising from the multifaceted responsibilities and pressures they face while working in a healthcare environment. This essay explores the sources and consequences of functional role stress for women working in hospitals in Hyderabad and suggests strategies to manage and mitigate this stress.

Functional role stress is a common phenomenon experienced by working women in hospital settings and can result from the unique demands and challenges associated with their roles. This type of stress can affect their well-being, job performance, and overall job satisfaction. Here are some of the key factors contributing to functional role stress among working women in hospitals:

- **Patient Care Responsibilities:** Healthcare professionals, including nurses and doctors, often bear the responsibility of providing direct patient care. This involves managing the physical and emotional needs of patients, which can be emotionally draining and stressful.
- **Long and Irregular Hours:** Many healthcare positions, especially those involving direct patient care, require long and irregular working hours. Shift work, including night shifts, can disrupt sleep patterns and lead to fatigue and stress.
- **Heavy Workloads:** Hospitals are fast-paced environments with high patient caseloads. Healthcare professionals often have heavy workloads, leaving them with limited time to provide individualized care.
- **Emergency Situations:** Hospitals frequently deal with critical and emergency cases. Healthcare workers must be prepared to respond to sudden crises, which can be highly stressful.
- **Complex Medical Cases:** The medical conditions and cases encountered in hospitals can be complex and challenging.

Treating patients with severe illnesses or traumatic injuries can be emotionally taxing.

- **Multitasking and Decision-Making:** Healthcare professionals must often multitask and make critical decisions quickly. The weight of these responsibilities can lead to stress and anxiety.
- **Emotional Toll:** Witnessing patient suffering and, in some cases, losing patients can take an emotional toll on healthcare professionals, leading to compassion fatigue and burnout.
- **Patient and Family Expectations:** Meeting the expectations and demands of patients and their families can be challenging, especially when they have high expectations for care and recovery.
- **Lack of Resources:** Shortages of staff, equipment, or resources can place added pressure on healthcare professionals, forcing them to do more with less.
- **Administrative and Documentation Burden:** Administrative tasks and extensive documentation are part of healthcare roles. The time spent on paperwork can detract from patient care and add to stress.
- **Team Dynamics:** Interactions and dynamics within healthcare teams can also contribute to functional role stress. Conflicts or communication challenges can affect job satisfaction.
- **Regulatory and Legal Pressure:** Healthcare professionals must adhere to numerous regulations and legal standards, which can create stress related to compliance and accountability.
- **Work-Life Balance:** Maintaining a work-life balance can be particularly challenging in healthcare due to demanding schedules. Finding time for personal life and self-care can be difficult.
- **Career Advancement Pressure:** The desire for career advancement and the pressure to continually update one›s skills and knowledge can contribute to stress.

- **Gender-Related Stress:** In some cases, working women in healthcare may experience stress related to gender bias or discrimination, affecting their confidence and well-being.

Consequences of Functional Role Stress:

- **Burnout and Mental Health Challenges**:
  Functional role stress can lead to burnout, emotional exhaustion, and mental health challenges for women working in hospitals. This can affect not only their well-being but also the quality of patient care they provide.
- **Impaired Work-Life Balance**:
  Balancing professional and personal life can become increasingly difficult, leading to strained relationships and limited time for self-care. An impaired work-life balance can exacerbate stress.
- **Career Advancement Challenges**:
  Women may find it challenging to advance in their healthcare careers due to the functional role stress they experience. Meeting the demands of their job while maintaining personal responsibilities can hinder professional growth.
- **Physical Health Implications**:
  Chronic stress can manifest in physical health issues, such as sleep disturbances, fatigue, and increased vulnerability to illnesses.

Strategies to Manage Functional Role Stress:

- **Time Management**:
  Implement effective time management strategies to allocate time for work, family, and self-care. Prioritizing tasks and setting boundaries can help alleviate stress.
- **Stress Management Techniques**:
  Learn stress management techniques such as mindfulness, relaxation exercises, and seeking social support to cope with the emotional challenges of the profession.

- **Work-Life Balance**:
  Strive to maintain a healthy work-life balance by setting realistic expectations and seeking support from family and peers. Balancing caregiving duties and professional responsibilities requires open communication and cooperation.
- **Professional Support**:
  Seek professional support, such as counseling or therapy, to address emotional stress and burnout. Many hospitals in Hyderabad offer employee assistance programs to support staff members.

Solution:

- **On-Site Childcare Services**:
  Establishing on-site childcare services within hospitals can be a game-changer for women workers. This initiative would alleviate the stress of finding suitable childcare arrangements and offer peace of mind, knowing that their children are nearby and well-cared for during their working hours. Hospital management should consider collaborations with reputable childcare providers to ensure the quality of these services.
- **Parental Leave and Supportive Policies**:
  Hospitals can revise their parental leave policies, providing extended leave options for both mothers and fathers. Additionally, supportive policies like remote work options, job-sharing, and phased return to work after maternity leave can make a significant difference. These policies should be clearly communicated to employees, encouraging women to take advantage of the support available to them.
- **Mental Health and Well-being Initiatives**:
  Hospitals should prioritize the mental health and well-being of their employees, particularly women who may experience heightened stress. Implementing mental health support programs, stress management workshops, and well-being

initiatives can help women cope with the demands of their profession while preserving their emotional and mental health.

- **Career Advancement Programs:**
  Hospital management can introduce career advancement programs tailored to the needs and aspirations of women working in healthcare. These programs should include mentorship opportunities, leadership training, and networking events. By offering clear pathways for career progression, hospitals can empower women to advance within their chosen field.
- **Employee Assistance Programs (EAPs):**
  Implementing EAPs can provide women workers with access to counseling, support for family-related issues, and stress management resources. These programs can assist in navigating the challenges of dual roles and offer practical guidance for managing role stress.

Conclusion:

Functional role stress is a significant challenge for women working in hospitals in Hyderabad. Recognizing the sources and consequences of this stress is the first step in addressing and mitigating it. By implementing time management strategies, stress management techniques, striving for work-life balance, and seeking professional support, women healthcare professionals can manage the demands of their roles more effectively. Additionally, support from employers and society to reduce gender role expectations can alleviate the unique stresses faced by women in the healthcare sector. Ultimately, it is essential to create a supportive and inclusive work environment that values the well-being of women workers and empowers them to provide quality patient care.

Role stress is a common challenge faced by women working in hospitals in Hyderabad. By implementing the suggested solutions, hospitals can create a supportive and inclusive work environment that enables women to manage their professional responsibilities while fulfilling their caregiving roles. Flexible scheduling, on-site childcare, improved parental leave policies, mental health initiatives, career advancement programs, and EAPs are essential components of this endeavor. These measures will not only enhance the well-being of women in healthcare but also contribute to a more diverse, equitable, and efficient healthcare system in Hyderabad. Ultimately, the advancement and well-being of women healthcare professionals benefit both the individual and the larger healthcare community.

PHYSICAL STRAIN

TABLE NO. 12

Physical Strain	Frequencies	Percentage
LOW	12	20.0
MEDIUM	48	80.0
Total	**60**	**100.0**

Level of Physical Strain is another important variable in this study. The above table shows that Physical Strain among working women in Private Sectors of Hyderabad. It shows that 12(20 percetnage) respondents are having low level of Physical Strain, 48(80 percentage) respondents are having medium level of depression and 15 (25 percentage) respondents are having high level of depression. It shows that among working women there is the level of depression is medium in this study.

Physical Strain:

Women working in hospitals in Hyderabad are at the forefront of healthcare, providing essential services to the city's residents. However, the demanding and physically strenuous nature of healthcare professions can take a toll on the well-being of these women. This essay explores the challenges related to physical strain that women working in Hyderabad hospitals encounter and the importance of addressing this issue to ensure their health and job satisfaction.

Working women in hospitals, particularly those in healthcare professions that involve patient care, can experience significant physical strain due to the nature of their work. Here are some of the physical strains they often encounter:

- **Lifting and Transferring Patients**: Nurses, nursing assistants, and other healthcare professionals frequently need to lift and transfer patients who may be immobile or require assistance. This can lead to musculoskeletal injuries, particularly in the back, shoulders, and wrists.
- **Standing for Extended Periods**: Many healthcare roles require long hours of standing or walking. This can result in foot, leg, and lower back discomfort, as well as conditions like varicose veins.
- **Repetitive Tasks**: Repetitive tasks such as administering medications, taking vital signs, or documentation can lead to overuse injuries, such as carpal tunnel syndrome and tendinitis.
- **Exposure to Infectious Diseases**: Healthcare workers, including women, are at risk of exposure to infectious diseases, which may necessitate the use of personal protective equipment (PPE). PPE can be uncomfortable and physically taxing, especially during extended shifts.
- **Shift Work**: Shift work, which is common in hospitals, can disrupt the body's natural circadian rhythms and lead to issues like sleep disturbances, fatigue, and overall physical discomfort.
- **Mobility and Agility**: In some healthcare roles, women may need to move quickly and be agile in emergency situations, which can be physically demanding and put strain on the body.
- **Handling Medical Equipment**: The operation of medical equipment and machinery may involve physical exertion and repetitive movements, contributing to strain and potential injuries.
- **Exposure to Chemicals and Hazardous Materials**: Some healthcare professionals work with chemicals and hazardous materials, which can have adverse physical effects if proper safety measures are not taken.

- **Infection Control Practices**: Maintaining strict infection control practices, such as frequent handwashing and glove use, can lead to skin issues and dryness, which can be physically uncomfortable.
- **Psychological and Emotional Strain**: The physical strain in healthcare can be exacerbated by the psychological and emotional toll of patient care. Stress, anxiety, and emotional exhaustion can manifest physically in the form of headaches, muscle tension, and other physical discomfort.

Challenges of Physical Strain Among Women Hospital Workers:

- **Long and Physically Demanding Shifts**: Healthcare jobs, particularly in hospitals, often require long and physically demanding shifts. Nurses, doctors, and other healthcare professionals may work extended hours, standing for most of their shifts, and performing tasks that require physical strength and endurance.
- **Lifting and Transferring Patients**: Women healthcare workers frequently engage in lifting and transferring patients, which can be physically demanding and pose a risk of injury. The weight of patients can strain the back, shoulders, and other muscles, leading to musculoskeletal issues.
- **Repetitive Tasks**: Repetitive tasks, such as administering medications, taking vitals, and handling medical equipment, can lead to physical strain and overuse injuries, particularly in the hands, wrists, and arms.
- **Work-Related Injuries**: The physically demanding nature of healthcare work can result in work-related injuries, including strains, sprains, and fractures, affecting women workers' well-being and their ability to perform their job effectively.
- **Inadequate Rest Breaks**: Insufficient rest breaks during long shifts can lead to fatigue and exacerbate physical strain, as women healthcare workers may not have enough time to recover and recharge.

- **Pregnancy and Parental Challenges**: For women healthcare workers who are pregnant or new mothers, the physical strain is heightened. Balancing the demands of pregnancy, childbirth, and childcare with the physical demands of the job can be particularly challenging.

Solution:

- **Proper Training**: Hospitals should provide comprehensive training on proper body mechanics and safe patient handling techniques to minimize the risk of injuries when lifting or transferring patients.
- **Ergonomic Equipment**: Hospitals should invest in ergonomic equipment and workstations to reduce physical strain. Adjustable chairs, computer stands, and other ergonomic tools can help improve working conditions.
- **Regular Breaks**: Ensuring that healthcare workers have adequate rest periods and breaks during their shifts can alleviate physical fatigue and reduce the risk of musculoskeletal injuries.
- **Staffing Levels**: Maintaining appropriate staffing levels is essential to distribute the physical workload evenly among healthcare workers and prevent excessive strain.
- **Injury Prevention Programs**: Hospitals should implement injury prevention programs, including exercises and stretches to strengthen muscles and prevent physical injuries.
- **Physical Well-being Support**: Hospitals can provide physical well-being support programs that include access to physiotherapy, counseling, and resources to cope with physical strain-related issues.

Conclusion:

The physical strain experienced by women working in hospitals in Hyderabad is a significant concern that requires attention. Ensuring the well-being of these dedicated healthcare professionals is vital for the effective functioning of the healthcare sector. By addressing physical strain through proper training, ergonomic improvements, appropriate staffing levels, and injury prevention programs, hospitals can create a safer and more supportive work environment. In doing so, they can help women workers maintain their physical health and job satisfaction while continuing to provide critical healthcare services to the community. Recognizing and addressing physical strain is an essential step in ensuring the physical well-being of women working in Hyderabad hospitals.

The physical strain faced by women working in Hyderabad hospitals is a genuine concern that needs to be addressed comprehensively. Hospitals can take proactive steps to reduce physical strain by implementing ergonomic practices, safe patient handling programs, and adequate staffing. Ensuring a supportive work environment and promoting a healthy work-life balance can help women healthcare workers maintain their physical well-being and continue delivering high-quality patient care. Recognizing and addressing the challenges of physical strain is essential to support the healthcare workforce and ensure the well-being of those who dedicate themselves to the health and well-being of others.

WORK LIFE BALANCE

- **Work-Life Balance:**
  Maintaining a work-life balance can be particularly challenging in healthcare due to demanding schedules. Finding time for personal life and self-care can be difficult.
- **Career Advancement Pressure:** The desire for career advancement and the pressure to continually update one›s skills and knowledge can contribute to stress.
- **Gender-Related Stress:** In some cases, working women in healthcare may experience stress related to gender bias or discrimination, affecting their confidence and well-being.

Consequences of Functional Role Stress:

- **Burnout and Mental Health Challenges:**
  Functional role stress can lead to burnout, emotional exhaustion, and mental health challenges for women working in hospitals. This can affect not only their well-being but also the quality of patient care they provide.
- **Impaired Work-Life Balance:**
  Balancing professional and personal life can become increasingly difficult, leading to strained relationships and limited time for self-care. An impaired work-life balance can exacerbate stress.
- **Career Advancement Challenges:**
  Women may find it challenging to advance in their healthcare careers due to the functional role stress they experience. Meeting the demands of their job while maintaining personal responsibilities can hinder professional growth.
- **Physical Health Implications:**
  Chronic stress can manifest in physical health issues, such as sleep disturbances, fatigue, and increased vulnerability to illnesses.

Strategies to Manage Functional Role Stress:

- **Time Management:**
  Implement effective time management strategies to allocate time for work, family, and self-care. Prioritizing tasks and setting boundaries can help alleviate stress.
- **Stress Management Techniques:**
  Learn stress management techniques such as mindfulness, relaxation exercises, and seeking social support to cope with the emotional challenges of the profession.
- **Work-Life Balance:**
  Strive to maintain a healthy work-life balance by setting realistic expectations and seeking support from family and peers.

Balancing caregiving duties and professional responsibilities requires open communication and cooperation.

- **Professional Support:**
  Seek professional support, such as counseling or therapy, to address emotional stress and burnout. Many hospitals in Hyderabad offer employee assistance programs to support staff members.

Solution:

- **On-Site Childcare Services:**
  Establishing on-site childcare services within hospitals can be a game-changer for women workers. This initiative would alleviate the stress of finding suitable childcare arrangements and offer peace of mind, knowing that their children are nearby and well-cared for during their working hours. Hospital management should consider collaborations with reputable childcare providers to ensure the quality of these services.
- **Parental Leave and Supportive Policies:**
  Hospitals can revise their parental leave policies, providing extended leave options for both mothers and fathers. Additionally, supportive policies like remote work options, job-sharing, and phased return to work after maternity leave can make a significant difference. These policies should be clearly communicated to employees, encouraging women to take advantage of the support available to them.
- **Mental Health and Well-being Initiatives:**
  Hospitals should prioritize the mental health and well-being of their employees, particularly women who may experience heightened stress. Implementing mental health support programs, stress management workshops, and well-being initiatives can help women cope with the demands of their profession while preserving their emotional and mental health.

- **Career Advancement Programs:**
  Hospital management can introduce career advancement programs tailored to the needs and aspirations of women working in healthcare. These programs should include mentorship opportunities, leadership training, and networking events. By offering clear pathways for career progression, hospitals can empower women to advance within their chosen field.
- **Employee Assistance Programs (EAPs):**
  Implementing EAPs can provide women workers with access to counseling, support for family-related issues, and stress management resources. These programs can assist in navigating the challenges of dual roles and offer practical guidance for managing role stress.

Conclusion:

Functional role stress is a significant challenge for women working in hospitals in Hyderabad. Recogni.

WORK LIFE BALANCE

TABLE NO. 13

Work Life Balance	Frequencies	Percentage
LOW	17	28.3
MEDIUM	20	33.3
HIGH	23	38.3
Total	60	100.0

Work Life Balance is another important variable in this study. The above table shows that Work Life Balance among working women in Private Sectors of Hyderabad. It shows that 17(28 percentage) respondents are having low Work Life Balance, 20(33 percentage) respondents are having medium level of Work Life Balance and 23 (38 percentage) respondents are having high level of Work Life Balance. It shows that among working women there is the level of Work Life Balance is high in this study.

CROSSTABLES

FAMILY SUPPORT * LEVEL OF WORK LIFE BALANCE

TABLE NO.1

FAMILY SUPPORT	WORK LIFE BALANCE			TOTAL
	LOW	MEDIUM	HIGH	LOW
LOW	9	5	LOW	9
	52.9%	25.0%		52.9%
MEDIUM	8	15	MEDIUM	8
	47.1%	75.0%		47.1%
TOTAL	**17**	**20**	TOTAL	**17**
	100.0%	**100.0%**		**100.0%**

CHI-SQUARE = .020

Family support and Level of Work Life Balance were divided into quartiles they were categorized into Low, Medium and High. Highlight of the table is where **women are having medium level of family support are having more work life balance.**

Family Support and Level of Work Life Balance significance tested with Chi-square which was found .02. Hence Hypothesis accepted.

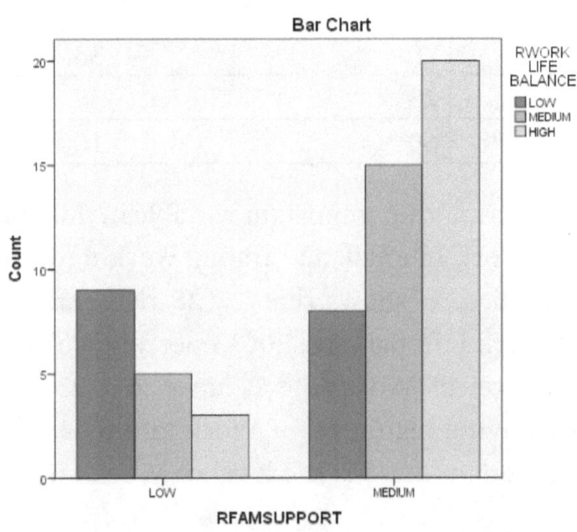

MANAGERIAL SUPPORT * LEVEL OF DEPRESSION

TABLE NO.2

C	DEPRESSION			TOTAL
	LOW	MEDIUM	HIGH	
LOW	8	7	2	17
	50.0%	24.1%	13.3%	28.3%
MEDIUM	0	22	4	31
	0.0%	75.9%	26.0%	51.7%
HIGH	8	0	9	12
	50.0%	0.0%	60.7%	20.0%
Total	**16**	**29**	**15**	**60**
	100.0%	**100.0%**	**100.0%**	**100.0%**

CHI-SQUARE = 000

Managerial support and Level of Depression were divided into quartiles they were categorized into Low, Medium and High. Highlight of the table is that where **women who are having high managerial support are having high level of Depression.**

Managerial Support and Depression significance tested with Chi-square which was found .00. Hence Hypothesis accepted.

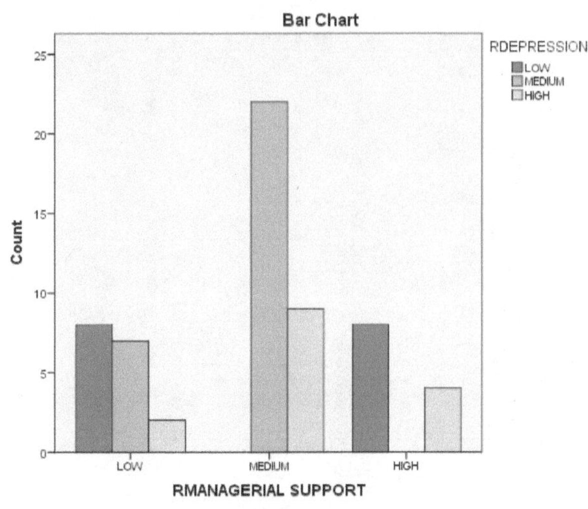

MANAGERIAL SUPPORT * WORK LIFE BALANCE

TABLE NO. 3

MANAGERIAL SUPPORT	WORK LIFE BALANCE			Total
	LOW	MEDIUM	HIGH	
LOW	17	0	0	17
	100.0%	0.0%	0.0%	28.3%
MEDIUM	0	20	11	31
	0.0%	100.0%	47.8%	51.7%
HIGH	0	0	12	12
	0.0%	0.0%	52.2%	20.0%
Total	**17**	**20**	**23**	**60**
	100.0%	**100.0%**	**100.0%**	**100.0%**

CHI-SQUARE = .000

Managerial support and Work Life Balance were divided into quartiles they were categorized into Low, Medium and High. Highlight of the table is that where **women who are having high managerial support are having high level of Work Life Balance.**

Managerial Support and Work life balance significance tested with Chi-square which was found .00. Hence Hypothesis accepted.

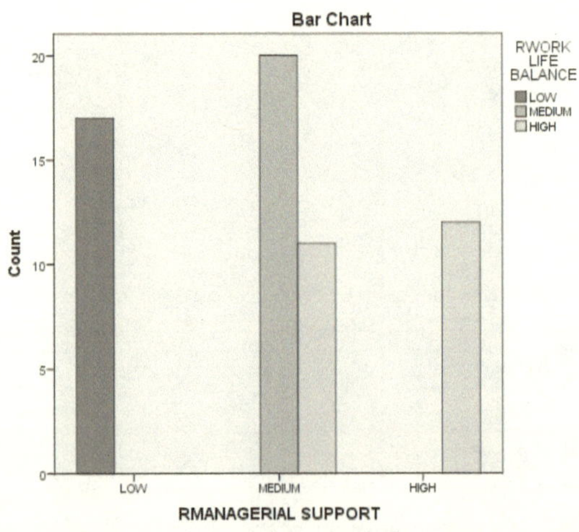

FAMILY SUPPORT* PHYSICAL STRAIN

TABLE NO. 4

FAMILY SUPPORT	PHYSICAL STRAIN		TOTAL
	LOW	MEDIUM	
LOW	2	15	17
	16.7%	31.2%	28.3%
MEDIUM	10	33	43
	83.3%	68.8%	71.7%
Total	**12**	**48**	**60**
	100.0%	**100.0%**	**100.0%**

CHI-SQUARE = .26

Family support and Physical Strain were divided into quartiles they were categorized into Low, Medium and High. Highlight of the table is that where **women who are having medium level of managerial support are having high level of Physical Strain.**

Managerial Support and Work life balance significance tested with Chi-square which was found .00. Hence Hypothesis accepted.

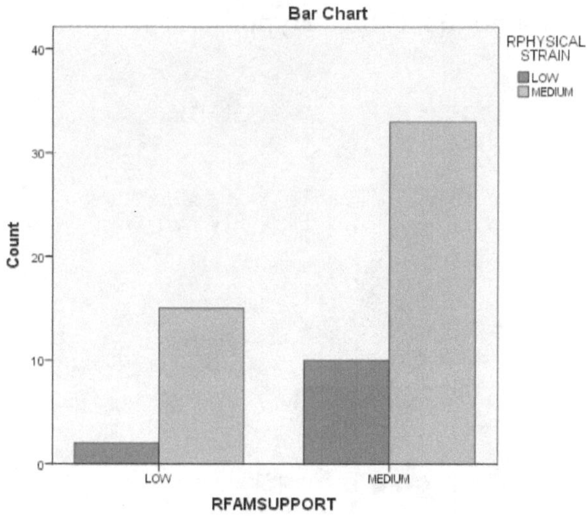

WORKING HOURS * LEVEL OF WORK LIFE BALANCE

TABLE NO.5

WORKING HOURS	WORK LIFE BALANCE			TOTAL
	LOW	MEDIUM	HIGH	
BELOW 7 YRS.	0	6	7	13
	0.0%	30.0%	30.4%	21.7%
8 HOURS TO 10 HOURS	15	14	16	45
	88.2%	70.0%	69.6%	75.0%
MORE THAN 10 HOURS	2	0	0	2
	11.8%	0.0%	0.0%	3.3%
TOTAL	**17**	**20**	**23**	**60**
	100.0%	**100.0%**	**100.0%**	**100.0%**

CHI-SQUARE=.02

Working Hours and Work Life Balance were divided into quartiles they were categorized into Low, Medium and High. Highlight of the table is that where **women who are having more working hours are having very low level of work life balance.**

Managerial Support and Work life balance significance tested with Chi-square which was found .02. Hence Hypothesis accepted.

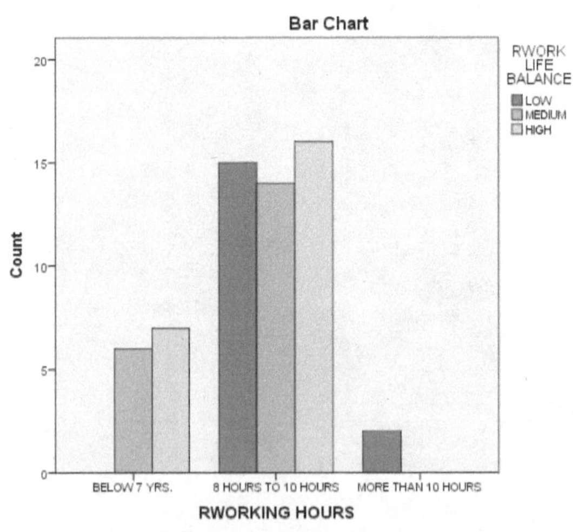

Findings and Conclusions

FINDINGS

- Middle age group respondents are more than Young and old age group of respondents in this study.
- Post Graduates are more than Graduates and others.
- Majority of the respondents are having one child
- Nuclear Family respondents are more than joint family.
- Majority of the respondents are working for 8 hours.
- Work Experience is minimum 6 years in majority of respondents.
- Family support is at medium level among more respondents.
- Functional Role Stress is at medium level among more respondents.
- Level of Depression among working married women is medium in private sectors of Hyderabad.
- Physical Strain among married working women is at medium level in Hyderabad Private Sectors.
- Work Life Balance Among married women is high in Private sectors of Hyderabad.

CONCLUSIONS

Work-life balance and organizational commitment are having the positive relationship. If nurses are having the goodwork-life balance, they are more committed to their organization. Hence, organizational should come forward tomake their life is important and give due weight to personal factors. The organization should treat that theiremployees are as clients. Even more in today ever challenges environment that demands are balancing of both workand life responsibilities. The organization actively seek to improve employee morale, commitment, and jobsatisfaction as well as aiming at the reduced source of stress both at work and home through work-life balance policies. It will improve their ability to become the employer of choice as well as retain talent. In the nursing profession, becoming the employer of choice means that hospital practices employment terms and conditions aregenerous enough to attract employees away from their competitors and keep their own employees from learning the hospital.

The hospital authorities need to consider the family aspect of their women employees, the steps like child care facilities, support for nurses who have aged parents, flexible working hours and to enhance their level of work-life balance maintenance. Management should take the necessary steps to spread awareness about their rights and work-life balance policies which is avail to them. The formal pragmatic strategy for communicating work-life policies should be essential. In Particular, to this group of employees, they are satisfied with the level of current life balance even though they had a little knowledge about it. Management should be capable to foresee the problems and cure it in advance. Irrespective of country or culture, t women face discrimination across the world. Management should be aware of the rights and privileges available to the women in particular and make them feel safe and secure at work sites. So management should take needful actions to prevent gender discrimination and behave in a compassionate way with special care and consideration to the need of the women employees. As far as women employees concerned they valued their organization utmost, management should take necessary steps to utilize their commitment in a favorable and healthy way which they can contribute the same for organizational, social development purpose. A scientific quality based selection of nursing employees in healthcare sector in general, ensure the quality service which will work as a mechanism to find solution for numerous work-life balance problems including reduce work overload, staff shortage and also reduce the level stress of the employees etc..

- Women Are having medium level of family support are having more work life balance.
- Women who are having high managerial support are having high level of Depression.
- Women who are having high managerial support are having high level of Work Life Balance.
- Women who are having medium level of managerial support are having high level of Physical Strain.
- Women who are having more working hours are having very low level of work life balance.

SUGGESTIONS

- In Private Sectors like Corporate hospitals the major problems faced by women is Night shifts. Due to their shift they were not able to concentrate on their child education and other problems which need to be addressed by them.
- In Corporate hospitals working hours are from 8 to 10 hours for Sisters and other staff. It need to be reduced to 7 hours then handing over will take one hour and the women can reach home as early as possible.
- Corporate management should go for Crenches for the children who are working in their hospitals. Because its an emergency based setting, where the women cannot surely leave the patient and go home to look after kids.
- Middle level staff should be appointed equally men and Women which can help the hospital and as well as the women.

www.ingramcontent.com/pod-product-compliance
Lightning Source LLC
LaVergne TN
LVHW041126150826
845673LV00007B/2196